World Wisdom
The Library of Perennial Philosophy

The Library of Perennial Philosophy is dedicated to the exposition of the timeless Truth underlying the diverse religions. This Truth, often referred to as the *Sophia Perennis*—or Perennial Wisdom—finds its expression in the revealed Scriptures as well as the writings of the great sages and the artistic creations of the traditional worlds.

An Illustrated Outline of Buddhism appears as one of our selections in the Perennial Philosophy series.

The Perennial Philosophy Series

In the beginning of the twentieth century, a school of thought arose which has focused on the enunciation and explanation of the Perennial Philosophy. Deeply rooted in the sense of the sacred, the writings of its leading exponents establish an indispensable foundation for understanding the timeless Truth and spiritual practices which live in the heart of all religions. Some of these titles are companion volumes to the Treasures of the World's Religions series, which allows a comparison of the writings of the great sages of the past with the perennialist authors of our time.

An Illustrated Outline of Buddhism

THE ESSENTIALS OF BUDDHIST SPIRITUALITY

William Stoddart

Foreword by
Joseph A. Fitzgerald

World Wisdom

An Illustrated Outline of Buddhism:
The Essentials of Buddhist Spirituality
© 2013 World Wisdom, Inc.

Book design by Clinton Minnaar and Stephen Williams

Cover and title page:
Bronze statue of the Great Buddha (*Daibutsu*)
of Kamakura, Japan, 1252

Library of Congress Cataloging-in-Publication Data

Stoddart, William.
An illustrated outline of Buddhism : the essentials of Buddhist spiritu-
ality / William Stoddart ; foreword by Joseph A. Fitzgerald.
    pages cm. -- (The perennial philosophy series)
Includes bibliographical references and index.
ISBN 978-1-936597-26-0 (pbk. : alk. paper) 1. Buddhism. I. Title.
BQ4022.S76 2013
294.3--dc23
                        2013006532

Printed on acid-free paper in South Korea

For information address World Wisdom, Inc.
P.O. Box 2682, Bloomington, Indiana 47402-2682
www.worldwisdom.com

CONTENTS

ACKNOWLEDGMENTS

For much helpful counsel and discussion, thanks are due to the late Ranjit Fernando, Alberto Martin, the late Richard Nicholson, Peter Oldmeadow, the late Marco Pallis, John Paraskevopoulos, and Gregory Phillips.

The author is indebted to Paulo Cesar Honorio for designing the four maps of the Buddhist areas of the world on pp. 52, 87, 108, and 111, and to Shrī Keshavram Iengar of Mysore for permission to reproduce his Sanskrit calligraphy on pp. 22 and 106.

Sitting Buddha, Sri Lanka, 8th-9th century

FOREWORD

The very small is as the very large when boundaries are forgotten.
The very large is as the very small when its outlines are not seen.
Seng ts'an, Third Patriarch of Ch'an (Zen) Buddhism[1]

A phenomenon of vast outward complexity calls for a synthesizing and delineating response, lest the forest's shape, for example, be lost sight of amid its countless trees. The present book is a highly successful response of this kind to the spiritual world of Buddhism. In a very small compass, Stoddart supplies a wealth of information, so much so, that one reviewer has called his book a "pocket encyclopedia"—not in the sense of a mere collection of facts, but in the infinitely more stimulating sense of a coordinated collection of key ideas or reference points to bear in mind along one's path of discovery.

This new illustrated edition, revised and enlarged a full generation after the first, provides a clear and succinct overview of Buddhist teachings and practices, from their origin in 531 B.C. when the Buddha attained Enlightenment, to their subsequent deployment and development at a variety of times and places, and among a variety of ethnicities. Special attention is given in this regard to the distinctive forms of Buddhism occurring, either historically or presently, in the regions of India, Tibet, China, Indo-China (including Burma, Thailand, Cambodia, and Laos), Korea, and Japan.

Stoddart's work also pays tribute to the overwhelming beauty of Buddhist art—amply confirmed by the rich selection of color reproductions in this volume—in a wide variety of schools.

An Illustrated Outline of Buddhism is thus not only useful, but moving and inspiring, and as such does full justice to a spiritual tradition that is unique and irreplaceable among the great religions of the world.

Joseph A. Fitzgerald

---

[1] Quoted in *Buddhist Texts Through the Ages*, ed. Edward Conze (New York: Philosophical Library, 1954), p. 298.

Opposite page: Shākyamuni Buddha at Vulture Peak Paradise, Central or Eastern Tibet

Meditating Buddha, Gupta Dynasty, Sārnāth, India

PREFACE

In the tumultuous 1950s and '60s, many of the discontented youth of the period came to the conclusion that the solution to their dissatisfaction must lie somewhere deeper than the immediately tangible realm. This did not turn them to Christianity, however, as they associated this religion with the complacent materialistic world of their parents, against which, precisely, they were rebelling.

Consequently, many turned their gaze to the Eastern religions, and in particular to Buddhism. Only a few, however, were serious enough to acquire a deep or sufficient knowledge of genuine Buddhist teachings. The majority had more enthusiasm than authenticity, and often, it seemed, filled their heads with a Buddhism of their own making. This was due not only to their lack of seriousness, but also to the unavailability, or inaccessibility, of easily assimilable and reliable information. It is this lack of information, and the resulting vagueness about Buddhism—which persists to the present day—that this book seeks to address.

As with the author's previous books in the "Outline" series, the purpose of *An Illustrated Outline of Buddhism: The Essentials of Buddhist Spirituality* is to provide a brief but comprehensive presentation of the religion concerned. It aims at summarizing its essential doctrines and practices, as well as noting its principal schools and cultural forms.

Because of Buddhism's several perspectives and ethnicities, it is difficult to write a "unitary" account of it without running the risk of over-simplification. In particular, every effort has been made to do justice to the *Hīnayāna* (*Theravāda*) and *Mahāyāna* views regarding the nature of Ultimate Reality, namely whether this be looked on as a Supreme State (*Nirvāna*) or a Supreme Being (variously referred to as *Ādi-Buddha*, *Vajradhara*, *Dharmakāya*, *Mahāvairochana*, or *Dainichi Nyorai*). Neither school has a watertight viewpoint, in that each perspective contains the other within itself—at least implicitly. This complex question is touched on briefly in chapters 1 and 8.

In this new edition, many illustrations of Buddhist art are provided, as well as tables of detailed information—which may be encountered in the course of reading about Buddhism. There is also a bibliography of suggested further reading.

William Stoddart

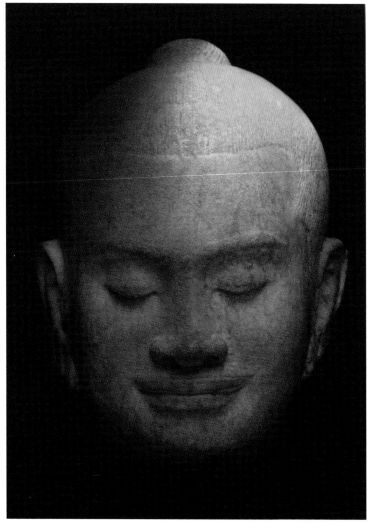

Buddha in the supreme state of *Nirvāna*, Angkor Wat, Cambodia

I teach two things, O disciples: suffering and release from suffering.

The Buddha (*Samyutta-Nikāya*, xxii, 86)

(1) Special Characteristics of Buddhism

Buddhism, at least in its *Theravāda* form,[1] is virtually unique amongst the religions of the world, in that it envisages "Ultimate Reality", not as a Supreme Being (Almighty God), but as a Supreme State (*Nirvāna*). Because of this seeming absence of the concept of God, at least in the manner envisaged by the Semitic religions, some have gone so far as to call Buddhism an "atheistic religion",—a contradiction in terms—, while others have alleged that it is not a religion at all, but a "philosophy".

Both of these views are incorrect. The "Supreme State" in Buddhism and the "Supreme Being" in the other religions are each expressions of the same transcendent Reality: That which is absolute, infinite, and perfect. Thus, the apparent difference between Buddhism and the other religions is in fact a difference of point of view or angle of vision. The essence of the matter is that Buddhism, like the other religions, has both its origin and its goal in the Eternal, the Sovereign Good. This is the nature of Ultimate Reality, and it is with Ultimate Reality that religion as such is concerned.

Buddhism is neither "atheistic" (in the usual connotation of this term), nor a "philosophy" (in the sense of being man-made); it is a revealed religion, coming from Ultimate Reality and leading to Ultimate Reality. There is no religion without revelation, that is to say: without revealed truth and without revealed sacramental means of liberation, deliverance, or salvation. These fundamentals are present in Buddhism, as in every other traditional and orthodox religion, and constitute its essence and its *raison d'être*.

Every religion—be it Semitic, Hindu, Buddhist, or Shamanist—takes account of the two divine aspects of Transcendence and Immanence. These can be expressed by different pairs of terms: Height and Depth, Above and Within, Remoteness and Proximity, Transcendent Being and Immanent Self, Divine Object and Divine Subject. One could say that religious law pertains to Transcendence, whereas the voice of conscience pertains to Immanence. Ultimate Reality is both Transcendence and Immanence, and every religion, in its theology and spirituality, expounds and has recourse to these two divine aspects in its own way. In the history of religions, and particularly in modern times, some heresies have had their origin in the neglect of one or other of these realities. In general terms, one might say that "transcen-

---

[1] For the two main schools of Buddhism, see p. 53.

dentism" without "immanentism" can lead to a kind of deism, whereas "immanentism" without "transcendentism" can lead to subjectivistic illusion. The majority of contemporary cults could be said to be "immanentist" heresies.

The Semitic religions—except occasionally in the context of their mysticism or spirituality—tend to emphasize the aspect of Transcendence (the Divine Being), whereas Buddhism tends to emphasize the aspect of Immanence (the Divine State). Nevertheless, the transcendentist—or "theistic"—perspective is also present in Buddhism, and characteristically comes to the fore in the *Mahāyāna* school. In his *Outlines of Mahāyāna Buddhism* (chapter IX), D. T. Suzuki writes: "God, or the religious Object of Buddhism, is generally called *Dharmakāya-Buddha* and occasionally *Vairochana-Dharmakāya-Buddha*; still another name for it is *Amitābha-Buddha* or *Amitāyus-Buddha*, the last two being mostly used by the followers of the *Sukhāvatī* ('Pure Land') sect of Japan and China." Suzuki states further: "The *Dharmakāya* assumes three essential aspects: intelligence (*prajñā*), love (*karunā*), and will (*pranidhānabala*)."[2]

Even in the *Hīnayāna* branch, the theistic perspective is by no means entirely absent. Moreover, it is an interesting and significant fact that, in several *Theravāda*[3] countries—Sri Lanka and Thailand, amongst others—the nearness of Hinduism served to reinforce the theistic component in the prevailing spiritual climate.

In summary: whereas most religions emphasize the "transcendent" aspect of Ultimate Reality, namely the Supreme Being or God, Buddhism characteristically emphasizes the "immanent" aspect, namely the Supreme State or *Nirvāna*. Nevertheless, Buddhism, in its total breadth, contains both aspects, the immanent and the transcendent, recognizing Ultimate Reality either as a Supreme State (*Nirvāna*) or as a Supreme Being (*Dharmakāya*). In either case, the essential nature of Ultimate Reality remains the same: it is absolute, infinite, and perfect. Thus, in its conception of Ultimate Reality, Buddhism is essentially in accord with every other world religion.

With this clarification in mind, let us formulate a definition of religion which will cover both Buddhism and the religions which are explicitly theistic.

---

[2] On *Dharmakāya*, see p. 50; on *Mahāvairochana* or *Ādi-Buddha*, see p. 72; on Amitābha, Amitāyus, and the "Pure Land" School, see pp. 55 and 79-80.

[3] *Theravāda* is the only surviving branch of *Hīnayāna* Buddhism. See p. 53.

There is an Unborn, Unoriginated, Uncreated, Unconditioned. If that Unborn, Unoriginated, Uncreated, Unconditioned were not, there could be no escape from this that is born, originated, created, conditioned. But because there is That which is Unborn, Unoriginated, Uncreated, Unconditioned, an escape from this that is born, originated, created, conditioned can be proclaimed.

Khuddaka-Nikāya, Udāna, 80ff

Bronze statue of the Buddha, Tibet, 15th century

Vajrachchedikā–Sūtra (the "Diamond Sūtra"), ink on paper, China, 868 A.D.

Frontispiece of the *Prajñā–Pāramitā–Sūtra*, Japan, late 12th century

*The mind endowed with intelligence is free from the intoxication
of sensuality, from the intoxication of things that change, from
the intoxication of ignorance.*

Dīgha-Nikāya

(2) What is Religion?

In terms of etymology, religion is that which binds, specifically, that which binds man to God. Religion engages man in two ways: firstly, by explaining the nature and meaning of the universe, or "justifying the ways of God to man" (this is theodicy); and secondly, by elucidating man's role and purpose in the universe, or teaching him how to liberate himself from its limitations, constrictions, and terrors (this is soteriology).

In the first place, religion is a doctrine of unity: God is one, and it is He who is the origin and final end of the universe and of man in it. Man, however, has become separated from God—through the "Fall" according to Christianity, through "ignorance" according to the Aryan religions. Consequently, religion is also a way of "return", a method of union. It is a sacramental path, a means of salvation.

Whatever they may be called, these two components are always present: theodicy and soteriology; doctrine and method; theory and practice; dogma and sacrament; unity and union.

Doctrine, or theory, concerns the mind (or, at the highest level, the "intellect", in the precise metaphysical sense of the Medieval *Intellectus*, the Greek *Nous*, or the Sanskrit *Buddhi*); method, or practice, concerns the will. Religion, to be itself, must always engage both mind and will.

The second, or practical, component of religion may be broken into two: namely, worship and morality. Worship, the sacramental element properly so-called, generally takes the form of participation in the revealed rites (public or private) of a given religion, with a view to conforming man's will to the norms of the Absolute, in other words, to the will of God. Morality, the social element, is "doing the things which ought to be done, and not doing the things which ought not to be done". Some of the contents of morality are universal: "thou shalt not kill", "thou shalt not steal", etc.; and some of the contents are specific to the religion in question: "thou shalt not make a graven image", "whom God hath joined together, let no man put asunder", etc.

We have thus reached the three elements which René Guénon considered to be the defining features of every religion: dogma, worship, and morality. When raised to a higher or more intense degree, namely that of spirituality or mysticism, they become, in the words of Frithjof Schuon: truth, spiritual way, and virtue. The purpose of a spiritual way is the assimilation or realization of divine truth—in other words effectively to know and love God.

The most important single point about religion is that it is not man-made. Religion is not invented by man, but revealed by God. Each religion is a unique revelation of Ultimate Reality. Divine revelation is a *sine quâ non*; without it, there is no religion, only man-made ideology, in which there is no guarantee of truth and above all no sacramental or salvational means.

The next important fundamental is tradition. Having once been revealed, religion is then handed down—unchanged in essence, but often increasingly elaborated in expression—from one generation to the next, by the power of tradition. And finally, closely linked with tradition, comes the attribute of orthodoxy, which is viewed as the principle of truth, or, at the practical level, the preservation of doctrinal purity.

In summary: religion's essential contents comprise dogma, worship, and morality; and religion's indispensable "container" or framework comprises revelation, tradition, and orthodoxy.

Page from the *Astasāhasrikā Prajñāpāramitā Sutra*,
depicting Green Tārā (*center*), Nepalese script, 11th century

It is difficult for pleasure-loving people to understand the causes of things.

The Buddha (*Majjhima-Nikāya*, ii, 32)

(3) What is Orthodoxy?

Nowadays, more often than not, orthodoxy is considered to be simply a form of intolerance: one set of people imposing their own views on others. In this connection, however, it is useful to recall the first item on the "Eightfold Path" of Buddhism: this is "right views" or "right thinking". It is obvious why "right thinking" should enjoy pride of place, for, both logically and practically, it is prior to "right doing". And what is the English word (derived from Greek) that signifies "right thinking"? None other than "orthodoxy".

To take the matter further: 2 + 2 = 4 is orthodox; 2 + 2 = 5 is unorthodox. Rather simple—but it also works the same way at much loftier levels. Another way of looking at it is this: even in the circumstances of today, many people still preserve the notion of "moral purity", and lay high value on it. Orthodoxy is "intellectual purity", and as such is an indispensable prelude to grace. Seen in this way—and far from "telling others what to believe"—orthodoxy is no more than a reference to the primacy and priority of truth. Orthodoxy, indeed, is the principle of truth that runs through the myths, symbols, and dogmas which are the very language of revelation.

Like morality, orthodoxy may be either universal (conformity to truth as such) or specific (conformity to the forms of a given religion). It is universal when it declares that God is uncreated, or that God is absolute and infinite. It is specific when it declares that Jesus is God (Christianity), or that God takes the triple form of Brahmā, Vishnu, and Shiva (Hinduism).

Departure from orthodoxy is heresy: either intrinsic (for example, atheism or deism), or extrinsic (for example, an adherent of a Semitic religion rejecting the divinities of the Hindu and Greek pantheons).

Orthodoxy is normal, heresy abnormal. This permits the use of a medical metaphor: the study of the various traditional orthodoxies is the affair of the religious physiologist, whereas the study of heresies (were it worthwhile) is the affair of the religious pathologist.

The notion of orthodoxy is particularly important in a world in which the great religions have become explicitly aware of one another, and in which their adherents often live cheek by jowl. It is similarly important in the field of comparative religion. This point has been well expressed by Bernard Kelly:

Confusion is inevitable whenever cultures based on profoundly different spiritual traditions intermingle without
rigid safeguards to preserve their purity. The crusader with
the cross emblazoned on his breast, the loincloth and spindle
of Mahātmā Gandhi when he visited Europe, are images of
the kind of precaution that is reasonable when traveling in a
spiritually alien territory. The modern traveler in his bowler
hat and pin stripes is safeguarded by that costume against any
lack of seriousness in discussing finance. Of more important
safeguards he knows nothing. The complete secularism of the
modern Western world, wherever its influence has spread, has
opened the floodgates to a confusion which sweeps away the
contours of the spirit. . . . Traditional norms . . . provide the
criteria of culture and civilization. Traditional orthodoxy is
thus the pre-requisite of any discourse at all between the Traditions themselves.[1]

Monks reciting the scriptures, Bodh-Gayā, northern India

---

[1] *Dominican Studies* (London), vol. 7, 1954, p. 256.

(4) Buddhism Amongst the World Religions

Before turning our attention to the internal features of Buddhism, it is important to know how to situate it amongst the religions of the world. The great religions fall into three fundamental categories: the Hyperborean shamanisms (comprising Confucianism, Taoism, and Shinto), the Aryan mythologies (comprising Hinduism, Buddhism, and the religion of Ancient Greece and Rome), and the Semitic monotheisms (comprising Judaism, Christianity, and Islam).

In terms of this classification, Buddhism (as an "Aryan mythology") falls in a different category from the religion best known to Westerners, namely Christianity. However, from another point of view, it can be said that the central role played by the person of the Buddha in Buddhism is analogous to the central role played by Christ in Christianity. This means that Buddhism can be classified, along with Hinduism and Christianity (and in contradistinction from Judaism and Islam) as "incarnationist". An important concomitant of incarnationism is iconography. In the incarnationist religions, iconography plays an essential sacramental role. Whereas Judaism and Islam are "iconoclastic" or "aniconic", Hinduism, Buddhism, and Christianity are "iconodulic". (See p. 23.)

It can also be said that, notwithstanding each religion being an original and distinct revelation in its own right, Buddhism emerged from the world of Hinduism, rather as Christianity emerged from the world of Judaism.

Furthermore, Buddhism (especially in its *Hīnayāna* or *Theravāda* form) is more or less unique in espousing the point of view that "Ultimate Reality" is a Supreme State, rather than a Supreme Being. As mentioned on p. 1, however, this is, on the one hand, a question of point of view, and on the other, a question of emphasis, as the "theistic" perspective is not only prominent in *Mahāyāna* Buddhism, but also by no means entirely lacking in *Theravāda* Buddhism.

Finally, it should be mentioned that Buddhism, like Christianity and Islam, is a "universal" religion, willingly accepting converts amongst "all nations", whereas Hinduism and Judaism are restricted to virtually one people. In general terms (and remembering that there are certain exceptions), one must be born a Hindu or a Jew, whereas anyone can become a Buddhist, Christian, or Muslim.

The basic classification of the religions referred to in the first paragraph is given in diagrammatic form on the following page.

Classification of the Religions

I. The Hyperborean Shamanisms

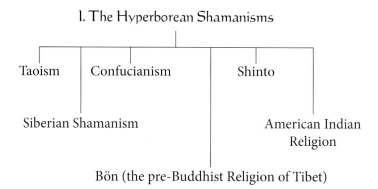

Taoism   Confucianism   Shinto

Siberian Shamanism   American Indian
                                   Religion

Bön (the pre-Buddhist Religion of Tibet)

II. The Aryan Mythologies

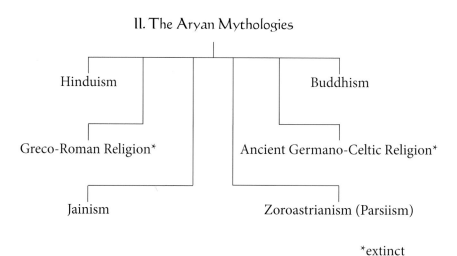

Hinduism   Buddhism

Greco-Roman Religion*   Ancient Germano-Celtic Religion*

Jainism   Zoroastrianism (Parsiism)

*extinct

III. The Semitic Monotheisms

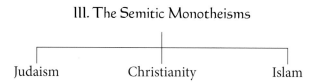

Judaism   Christianity   Islam

China's Three Messengers:
(*left*) Confucius (551-479 B.C.), (*right*) Lao Tzu (604-531 B.C.),
and (*center*) the Buddha (563-483 B.C.)

It is compassion that constitutes the very heart of the Buddha.
Hōnen

(5) Life of the Buddha, Origin of Buddhism

The religion of Buddhism derives from the one who was called the *Buddha* (Sanskrit for "Enlightened" or "Awakened"). His family name was Gautama, and his given name was Siddhārtha. Siddhārtha Gautama was born about 563 B.C., in the Lumbinī Grove near Kapilavastu, in what is now Nepal. His father, Shuddhōdana, was raja of the Aryan Shākya tribe. His mother, Māyā, was the daughter of the raja of the neighboring Koliyan tribe. Their families belonged to the Hindu *kshatriya* caste (i.e. the royal, aristocratic, or "warrior" caste). The dormition of Queen Māyā took place seven days after she gave birth: "having beheld the glory of her new-born child, she could not sustain the joy he brought her, and, so as not to die of it, she ascended into Heaven" (The *Buddha-Charita* of Ashvaghosha, II, 18).

When Siddhārtha Gautama was sixteen years old, he was married to his cousin Yashodharā. Gautama lived happily with his wife in princely luxury, free from the knowledge of care and want. After ten years of marriage, they had a son who was named Rāhula.

Siddhārtha Gautama's father had ordered that, whenever he rode out in his chariot from the palace into the city, no aged, no sick, and no funeral procession should be in sight—only young and beautiful people. Nevertheless, in spite of this precaution, when he was twenty-nine years old, he came face to face with human suffering. The God Indra himself appeared before his chariot four times: in the forms of an old man, a sick man, a dead man, and a monk. The first three symbolically revealed to him the nature of the world, and in the fourth he saw a symbol prefiguring a solution. Profoundly concerned with the problem of suffering and the fragility of earthly happiness, he returned to his palace a changed man. That very night, in a spirit of renunciation, he left his sleeping wife and child, taking with him only his charioteer, Channa, and his horse, Kanthaka. He miraculously passed through the palace gates which his father had ordered to be locked. When far from the city, he donned a hermit's robe and bade Channa take his horse and fine garments back to the palace. He shaved his head and became a wandering mendicant.

For six years Siddhārtha Gautama sought a solution. He turned first to the Hindu ascetics Ārāda Kālāma and Udraka Rāmaputra, but was not satisfied with their teachings. Then he undertook a long period of solitary mortification in a forest. He acquired a reputation for sanctity, and five brahmin hermits attached themselves to him. He attained

Opposite page: Shākyamuni Buddha with scenes from his life, Tibet, 15th century no enlightenment, however, and finally abandoned his mortification and began to eat normally. Thereupon the five hermits were disappointed and left him.

Gautama walked along the banks of the river Nairanjara and, at a place not far from the city of Gayā, sat down under a pipal tree—the sacred Bodhi-tree (*Ficus religiosa*) or "Tree of Enlightenment". He vowed not to move thence until he had attained enlightenment. He remained there for some weeks, and was given food by Sujātā, the daughter of a nearby farmer, who had first mistaken him for a sylvan deity. Māra, the evil one, came to him, and attacked him with storms, darkness, flood, and fire. Gautama remained unmoved, and Māra fled. As the day wore on, his mind became ever clearer, a great peace came over him, and the significance of all things became apparent. Day and night passed and, just before dawn, there came perfect knowledge (*bodhi*). Prince Siddhārtha Gautama had become *Buddha*, the "Enlightened One". It is in this descent of "enlightenment" upon the Buddha—about 531 B.C.—that the Buddhist revelation has its origin. The place where it occurred was henceforth known as Bodh-Gayā.

The Buddha remained under the Bodhi-tree for forty-nine days, fearing that the content of his Enlightenment could not be expressed in words or otherwise conveyed to men. But the God Brahmā himself descended from Heaven, declared to him that the world left to itself was lost, and bade him preach to those who wished to be saved. The Buddha then arose and made his way to Isipatana, the "Deer Park" at Sārnāth near the holy city of Benares, where he again met the five brahmin hermits who had deserted him. They had not found liberation through their asceticism and now entreated the radiant and enlightened Buddha to instruct them. It was to them that he preached his famous first sermon, the first "Setting in Motion of the Wheel of the Law" (*Dharmachakra Pravatana*),[1] which included the "Four Noble Truths" and the "Eightfold Path" (see p. 35). The hermits and others accepted the Buddha's teaching and became his followers. Then he made a return visit to Kapilavastu, where he converted his father, wife, and son, as well as many members of the court.

For forty-five years, the Buddha preached all over the kingdom of Māgadha (corresponding approximately to what is now Bihar). His

---

[1] It is said that the "Wheel of the Law" was set in motion three times: in the First Sermon (which gave rise to early or primitive Buddhism), in the origin of the *Mahāyāna*, and in the origin of the *Vajrayāna*. (See pp. 53-55.)

Mahābodhi Temple, Bodh-Gayā, northern India,
site of the Buddha's Enlightenment

teaching became known as the *Dharma* (the "Law").[2] He established an order of monks and an order of nuns, together known as the *Sangha* (the Buddhist community). The legacy of Buddhism is thus traditionally said to consist of the "Three Jewels" (Sanskrit: *Triratna*/Pali: *Tiratana*): the *Buddha*, the *Dharma*, and the *Sangha*. They are also known as the "Three Refuges" (*tri-sharana/ti-sarana*), in view of the fundamental Buddhist prayer: "I take refuge in the *Buddha*, the *Dharma*, and the *Sangha*". (See next page.)

From the earliest days—up to present times—the Buddhist community has been divided into monks (*bhikshus/bhikkus*) and householders (*upāsaka*). The monastic discipline is naturally more strict, but both monks and householders are subject to the basic tenets and practices of Buddhism. From a more profound point of view, the fundamental spiritual division in Buddhism (as indeed in all religions) is the one between the "sincere" or totally committed (*āryashrāvaka/ariyasāvaka*, literally "noble hearer") and the "hypocrite" or less-than-totally committed (*puthujjana*). This "spiritual" distinction completely cuts across the merely "social" distinction between monk and layman.[3]

The Buddhist Scriptures are voluminous and record the teachings—sermons, sayings, and actions—of the Buddha. The earliest comprehensive recension is the Pali Canon (Pali being a North Indian language related to Sanskrit), which was codified at the First Buddhist Council in 480 B.C. The Pali Canon is also known as the *Tripitaka/Tipitaka* (the "Three Baskets") and comprises the *Vinaya Pitaka* (the "Discipline Basket"), the *Sutta Pitaka* (the "Instruction Basket"), and the *Abhidhamma Pitaka* (the "Metaphysical Basket").

The source of these Scriptures was the prodigious memory of the Buddha's closest disciples: Upāli's recall was the source of the *Vinaya Pitaka* and Ānanda's was the source of the *Sutta Pitaka*. The long *Sutta Pitaka* is divided into five "groups" or *nikāyas*: *Dīgha, Majjhima, Samyutta, Anguttara*, and *Khuddaka*. The *Khuddaka-Nikāya* includes the well-known treatise, the *Dhammapada* or "Footprints of the Law".

Essentially the same canon also exists in Sanskrit, as do important later Scriptures, pertaining particularly to *Mahāyāna* Buddhism, such as the *Prajñā-Pāramitā-Sūtra* (the "Supreme Wisdom Sūtra"), the

---

[2] *Dharma* also has the meanings of "inner law", "vocation", "true nature", "primordial norm".

[3] See *Divine Revelation in Pali Buddhism* by Peter Masefield, chap. 1 (London: Allen & Unwin; Colombo: Sri Lanka Institute of Traditional Studies, 1986).

Vajrachchedikā-Sūtra (the "Diamond Sūtra"), the *Sukhāvatī-Sūtra* (the "Pure Land Sūtra"), the *Saddharma-Pundarīka-Sūtra* (the "Lotus of the Good Law Sūtra"), and the *Lankāvatāra-Sūtra* (the "Manifestation in Lankā Sūtra").

About 483 B.C., at the age of eighty years, the Buddha died at Kushinagara (the present-day Kasia, near Gorakhpur, in Uttar Pradesh). This was his final "expiration" (*Parinirvāna*). His last words were: "Decay inheres in all created things. With clear mind give due heed to your salvation."

Page from the *Prajñā-Pāramitā-Sūtra*, depicting Shākyamuni Buddha (*left*) and Prajñāpāramitā (*right*), Tibetan script, 13th century

Namo tassa Bhagavato Arahato Sammā-sambuddhassa!
Homage to the Blessed, the Worthy, the Fully-Enlightened!

Buddham saranam gacchāmi;
To the Buddha, the refuge, I go;

Dhammam saranam gacchāmi;
To the Dharma, the refuge, I go;

Sangham saranam gacchāmi.
To the Sangha, the refuge, I go.

Ti-sarana-gamana

The Blessed One said: "Know, Varatha, that from time to time a Tathāgatha *(a 'Thus-Gone' or a 'Fully-Arrived') is born into the world, a fully Enlightened One, blessed and worthy, abounding in wisdom and goodness, happy with the knowledge of the worlds, unsurpassed as a guide to erring mortals, a teacher of gods and men, a Blessed Buddha. He thoroughly understands this universe, as though he saw it face to face. . . . The Truth does he proclaim, in both its letter and its spirit—lovely in its origin, lovely in its progress, lovely in its consummation. A higher life does he make known, in all its purity and perfection."*

Tevijja-Sutta

Shākyamuni Buddha with disciples Mahākāshyapa and Ānanda,
ink and color on silk, Ming Dynasty, China, c. 15th-16th century

(6) Some Early Buddhist Figures

Mahākāshyapa (sixth-fifth centuries B.C.)

After his enlightenment, the Buddha proceeded to Rājagriha where King Bimbisāra put the Bamboo Grove (*Venuvana*) at his disposal. While there, Shāriputra and Maudgalyāyana (devotees of the Hindu teacher Sanjayin) became acquainted with one of the Buddha's disciples, who conveyed to them the essence of his master's doctrine in the famous verse:

> Of all things proceeding from a cause, the cause has been shown by Him-thus-come; and their cessation too the Great Pilgrim has declared.
>
> *Saddharma-Pundarīka-Sūtra*, 27/*Mahāvagga*, 1:23

This caused the two immediately to convert, and they soon became leading disciples of the Buddha. In images, they are often depicted on either side of the Buddha. They died shortly before the Buddha himself.

The group at the Bamboo Grove was also joined by the brahmin Pippali, later known as Kāshyapa, who likewise converted and in due course became the Buddha's principal disciple. Following the Buddha's death, Kāshyapa took over the leadership of the community (*sangha*). Kāshyapa (called Mahākāshyapa, "the great Kāshyapa") had been the only disciple to understand the Buddha's famous "flower sermon". It is said that once the god Brahmā appeared to a gathering of the disciples on Mount Gridhrakūta ("Vulture Peak") near Rājagriha and asked the Buddha to expound the *dharma*. The Buddha, instead of giving a discourse, merely held up a flower. None of those present understood what this meant, except Kāshyapa, who responded with a smile. The Buddha then said: "The true *dharma* cannot be expressed through words or letters; it is a special transmission outside the written scriptures; this transmission I entrust to Kāshyapa." It was thus that Mahākāshyapa became the first Indian patriarch of *Dhyāna*, *Ch'an*, or *Zen* Buddhism. Starting with him, the supra-formal *dharma* was transmitted by twenty-eight Indian patriarchs down to Bodhidharma, a South Indian prince, who went to China in 520 A.D. and became the first patriarch of *Ch'an* in that country. (See p. 53.)

Ānanda (sixth-fifth centuries B.C.)

Ānanda was a cousin of the Buddha, and another of his leading disciples. It was at his intercession that the Buddha consented to the founding of an order of nuns. His extraordinary recall of the Buddha's discourses was the basis of the codification of the earliest Buddhist Scriptures. Ānanda became the second Indian patriarch of *Dhyāna* Buddhism. In the main hall of many Chinese monasteries, there is an image of the Buddha, with Kāshyapa on his right and Ānanda on his left.

Ashoka (third century B.C.)

Ashoka, a scion of the Hindu Mauryan Dynasty, was king of the ancient North Indian kingdom of Māgadha (corresponding approximately to the modern Bihar), who converted to Buddhism. Following his warlike earlier years, when he conquered much territory and acquired dominion over the greater part of the Indian sub-continent, he became one of the greatest and most saintly rulers in Indian history; his avowed intention was to establish a "reign of *dharma*". He was the most benevolent of monarchs, watching carefully over the well-being of his subjects, and maintaining friendly relations with neighboring states. His son Mahinda was instrumental in taking Buddhism to Ceylon (now Sri Lanka), and under Ashoka's influence Buddhism also spread in Burma. His famous "edicts" enshrine the precepts that he propagated. For example: "Never think or say that your own religion is best; never denounce the religion of others. He who does reverence to his own sect, while disparaging the sects of others . . . and with intent to enhance the glory of his own sect, in reality by such conduct inflicts the severest injury on his own sect."

Milinda (c. first century B.C.-first century A.D.)

Milinda is usually identified with the Greco-Indian King Menander, who, around the turn of the millennium, conquered a large tract of Northern India. Milinda posed a number of questions regarding Buddhism to the monk Nāgasena, and the latter's answers are said not only to have converted Milinda to Buddhism, but henceforth, in the form of the treatise *Milindapañha* ("The Milinda Questions") became an important source of *Theravāda* perspectives on some of the central theses of Buddhism, such as *karma* and *anātmā*.

Ashvaghosha (first-second centuries A.D.)

Ashvaghosha was born into a brahmin family, but was converted to Buddhism by a Buddhist monk. He wrote in Sanskrit, and was a poet, dramatist, and musician. He was revered as a "sun that illuminates the world". Originally from Eastern India, he settled in Benares. He was the earliest and greatest philosopher of the Northern School of Buddhism, and reputedly the author of the classic work "A Treatise on the Awakening of Faith in the *Mahāyāna*" (*Mahāyāna-Shraddhotpāda-Shāstra*). This was translated into Chinese in the sixth century, and is renowned in China and Japan. He wrote in verse a life of the Buddha (*Buddha-charita*) from his birth to his *Parinirvāna* ("final expiration"). He was the 12th Indian patriarch of *Dhyāna* Buddhism, and probably the guru of Nāgārjuna, the 14th patriarch.

Nāgārjuna (second-third centuries A.D.)

Nāgārjuna was one of the most celebrated of Buddhist scholars and teachers. He was born of a brahmin family in South India, and early in life acquired great learning. He converted to Buddhism, took monastic vows, and mastered the *Hīnayāna* canon. Later he went to the Himalayas, where he assimilated the *Mahāyāna* sūtras. He thus encompassed in his person both the *Hīnayāna* and the *Mahāyāna* teachings. He was outstanding as a philosopher, and the doctors of the Buddhist university of Nālandā in Bihar claim him as their forefather. He was a prolific author, much of his work interpreting and expounding the *Prajñā-Pāramitā-Sūtra*. He was the founder of the *Mādhyamika* ("Middle Way") school of *Mahāyāna* Buddhism and also the 14th Indian patriarch of *Dhyāna* or Zen.

Vasubandhu (fourth-fifth centuries A.D.)

Vasubandhu was born in Purushapura (now Peshāwar) in the ancient north-west Indian province of Gandhāra. He lived for some years in Kashmir and died in Ayodhyā in what is now Uttar Pradesh. He and his brother Asanga, along with Maitreyanātha, were the founders of the *Yogāchāra* (or *Vijñānavāda*) school of *Mahāyāna* Buddhism, for which one of the most important scriptures is the *Lankāvatāra-Sūtra*. (*Yogāchāra* = "Teaching of Union"; *Vijñānavāda* = "The Way of Discrimination".) Vasubandhu was the 21st Indian patriarch of *Dhyāna*.

Buddhaghosha (fourth-fifth centuries A.D.)

Buddhaghosha was born into a brahmin family who lived near Bodh-Gayā. He converted to Buddhism and migrated to Ceylon, where he took up residence in the Mahāvihāra monastery at Anurādhapura. He identified completely with the *Theravāda* school and wrote important commentaries in Pali on the *Tipitaka*. His main work was "The Way of Purity" (*Visuddhi-Magga*).

Bodhidharma (fifth-sixth centuries A.D.)

Bodhidharma was the son of a South Indian king. He converted to Buddhism, and was the disciple of Prajñādhara, the 27th Indian patriarch of *Dhyāna* Buddhism. He eventually became his successor, the 28th patriarch. In 520 A.D. he went by ship from India to China. There he traveled widely, teaching the Buddhist doctrines. He was received in audience by the Emperor Wu-ti of the Liang Dynasty, who was a patron of Buddhism. Bodhidharma became the first patriarch of *Ch'an* (*Dhyāna*) Buddhism in China. He remained in that country until his death.

ॐ येधर्मा हेतुप्रभवा हेतुं तेषां तथागतो ह्यवदत् ।
तेषां च यो निरोध एवंवादि महाश्रमणः॥ स्वाहा॥

Sanskrit Buddhist text in Devanāgarī script
(calligraphy by Shrī Keshavram Iengar):
"Of all things springing from a cause,
the cause has been shown by him 'Thus-come';
and their cessation too the Great Pilgrim has declared."
Saddharma-Pundarīka-Sūtra, 27

(7) Buddhist Art

It is not the purpose of this book to deal with the immense, variegated, and wonderful world of Buddhist art,[1] but, in view of its importance, passing mention should perhaps be made of three important early schools.

Firstly it must be understood that, like all sacred art, Buddhist art is of supernatural origin: it derives from the Buddha himself, and is an integral part of the Buddhist sacramental system. It is said in the *Divyāvadāna* that King Rudrāyana (Udāyana) of Kaushāmbī sent painters to the Buddha in order to paint an image of him which the faithful could venerate in his absence. When the painters failed to capture his essential form, the Buddha said that this was due to their spiritual lassitude. He then ordered that a canvas be brought to him, and he projected his similitude upon it.

According to the seventh century Chinese monk Hsüan-Tsang, King Udāyana had an image of the Buddha made in sandalwood during the latter's life-time and this became the prototype or model for innumerable later copies.[2]

Buddhism, therefore, like Hinduism and Christianity, is "incarnationist" and "iconodulic".[3] In this it contrasts with Judaism and Islam, which are "non-incarnationist" and "iconoclastic". According to Buddhist doctrine, "the Buddhas also teach by means of their superhuman beauty". This explains why the magnificent iconography of Buddhism, a veritable "outward sign of inward grace", plays such an important sacramental role. An icon (*pratīka*) "objectivizes" a transcendent principle which, in the worshiper, becomes a "subjective" state. In this way, the icon is a vehicle of spiritual realization. The same idea finds expression in the Platonic doctrine that "beauty is the splendor of the true": truth's radiant beauty, made visible in sacred art, has the power to transform hearts and save souls.

---

[1] For an excellent exposition of the spiritual meaning of Buddhist art, see *Sacred Art in East and West* by Titus Burckhardt (Bloomington, IN: World Wisdom, 2001).

[2] See *Elements of Buddhist Iconography* by Ananda Coomaraswamy (Cambridge, MA: Harvard University Press, 1935), p. 6.

[3] In Christian theology, a distinction is made between *latreia* ("worship"—due only to God) and *dulia* ("veneration"—due to saints, relics, and icons). Hence "iconodulia" (which is legitimate) and "idolatry" (which is illegitimate).

In statues and paintings, the Buddha is always depicted in a particular posture or with a particular gesture of the hands. These bodily poses or attitudes are known as *mudrās*, and derive from the Hindu tradition, having been revealed in the *Bharata-Nātya-Shāstra*. They symbolically represent certain aspects of the Buddha's actions (e.g. preaching), doctrines (e.g. the Four Noble Truths), or radiance (e.g. protective blessing). They may also represent spiritual perfections or inward states of soul. In the case of Buddhist worshipers, *mudrās* may sometimes accompany the recitation of prayers or *mantras*. Lovers of Hindu dancing (*bharata natyam*) will be aware that *mudrās* are the very essence of that sacred art.

The Scriptures of several religions tell us that, over and above sacred art—and prior to it—, God's truth is manifested first and foremost in the beauty of nature. This amounts to a veritable natural sacrament, and it is one to which the Buddhists of Japan—amongst others—are particularly sensitive.

*
*   *

Let us now come to the three important early schools of Buddhist art: Between the 1st and 3rd centuries A.D., Mathurā (in Uttar Pradesh) was a center of Buddhist art and culture. It was at Mathurā—and also at Gandhāra—that the earliest extant stone statues of the Buddha were found. Because of this, art historians have mostly taken the view that, before this period, Buddhist art consisted only of symbols, such as a wheel, a throne, a tree, etc. However, it is recorded that statues of the Buddha were made from his life-time onwards, but being in wood, these have not endured. In the art of Mathurā, the human form is full, rounded, and fluid without being heavy.

In the fourth century B.C., the north-west Indian province of Gandhāra was conquered by Alexander the Great. When, at the beginning of the Christian era, the inhabitants of Gandhāra became Buddhists, the artistic legacy of Alexander, coupled with continuing trading links with the Greco-Roman world, imposed on the Buddhist art of Gandhāra, from the second to the fifth century A.D., a markedly Hellenistic stamp—a strange anomaly in the history of Buddhist art. The figures in the art of Gandhāra tend to be slender and elegant.

More important—and more seminal—in the evolution of Buddhist art was the amazing flowering that took place during the long

Buddha seated on a lion throne, Mathurā, India, 2nd century A.D.

Scene from the life of the Buddha, Gandhāra, late 2nd to early 3rd century A.D.

Carvings from the Great Stūpa of Sānchī, central India:
Buddha represented as a *stūpa* (*left*), as the sacred tree (*center*), and as the Wheel of the Law (*right*)

The Great Stūpa of Sānchī, central India

Gupta Dynasty (fourth-seventh centuries A.D.) in the North Indian kingdom of Māgadha and its considerable territorial extensions. Art of the Gupta period is in evidence at Ajantā, Ellorā, Sānchī, and Sārnāth. In a way it is a synthesis of the two earlier styles: in it fluidity and elegance are combined. Gupta art had a formative influence on virtually all subsequent developments in both Hindu and Buddhist art in India and beyond.

*
* *

In Buddhist architecture, one encounters *stūpa*s (memorials, tombs, or reliquaries) and *vihāra*s (resting-places or monasteries). The pagodas of China, Korea, and Japan were developed from the original Indian *stūpa*s.

An art form common in Tibet is that of the *t'hanka*, a painted scroll on cotton or silk. The paintings usually portray Buddhas and Bodhisattvas but may also portray a *mandala*, a symbolic "diagram" used as a support for meditation.

The Buddhas save human beings in four ways: (1) by their oral teaching, as set out in the twelve categories of Buddhist Scriptures; (2) by their physical traits of supernatural beauty; (3) by their marvelous powers, their properties, and their transformation; (4) by their Names, which when uttered by men remove all obstacles and assure rebirth in the presence of the Buddha.

T'ao-ch'o, The Book of Peace and Happiness

Gilded bronze *stūpa*, Mongolia, late 17th century

The Golden Pavilion, Kyoto, Japan, late 14th century

T'hanka depicting a *stūpa* surrounded by eight Bodhisattvas, Tibet, 18th century

T'hanka of the *Kalachakra mandala*, Tibet, late 15th century

The Four Brahma-Viharas

The "Four Divine Dwellings" or "Cardinal Virtues" of Buddhism

(1) loving-kindness (*maitrī*)

(2) compassion (*karunā*)

(3) joy (*muditā*)

(4) serenity (*upekshā*)

Bodhisattva Padmapani, "bearer of the lotus",
Ajanta Caves, India, 6th century A.D.

(8) The Nature and the Teachings of Buddhism

Buddhism emerged from Hinduism, rather as Christianity emerged from Judaism. Christianity mediated Abrahamic monotheism to the world of the Gentiles, just as Buddhism mediated the wisdom of the Vedas to almost the whole of Eastern Asia. Christianity and Buddhism are nevertheless completely original as revelations in their own right, and not mere adaptations or developments of the respective antecedent revelations.

Just as Christianity dispensed with the Jewish law (in the name of worshiping God "in spirit and in truth"), so Buddhism dispensed with the formal institutionalization of caste (in the name of a purely spiritual brotherhood and sisterhood).

As explained in chapter 1, in *Theravāda* Buddhism the Highest (or "Divine") Reality is envisaged not as a Supreme Being (Almighty God), as it is in most other religions, but as a Supreme State (*Nirvāna*). *Nirvāna* literally means "extinction", and this refers to the extinction of all that is fallen, corrupt, finite, and impermanent. Buddhism (with the exception of some *Mahāyāna* currents) does not look on the world as a theophany, but as an exile; it does not look on it under its positive aspect of symbol or support, but under its negative aspect of corruption and temptation—and so of suffering (*duhkha*). It is on this basis that Buddhism, characteristically, expresses a positive reality in negative terms: the intention is to underline the fact that *Nirvāna* (a negation of the negative) is Reality: absolute, infinite, and perfect. In like manner, Ultimate Reality is also called *Shūnyatā* ("Void"), that is to say, it is empty of the ephemeral pseudo-plenitude of the world. Significantly, one of the titles of the Buddha is *Shūnyamūrti*, "Manifestation of the Void". This title is a clear indication of the Buddha's role as *Logos* or *Avatārā*.

In Buddhism, Ultimate Reality is also referred to, in different contexts, as *Dharma* ("Law"), *Bodhi* ("Awakening", "Enlightenment", "Knowledge"), and *Ātmā* ("Self"). Ultimate or Divine Reality—and this is particularly the case in *Mahāyāna* Buddhism—is also regarded as a Supreme Being.[1]

---

[1] Relevant here, and applicable in all religions, is the theological distinction between God Transcendent, the Divine Being or "Object" (*Brahma, Mahāvairochana, Jehovah, Allāh*) and God Immanent, the Divine Self or "Subject" (*Ātmā*).

The foregoing makes it clear why, whether Ultimate Reality be primarily viewed as a Supreme State (*Nirvāna*) or a Supreme Being (*Dharmakāya* or *Mahāvairochana*), it is erroneous to call Buddhism "atheistic". Ultimate Reality, as envisaged by Buddhism (be it conceived as "State" or "Being"), is absolute, infinite, and perfect, and these are precisely the transcendent categories that atheism denies.

Likewise, it is incorrect to call Buddhism a "philosophy" (in the modern sense of this word), rather than a "religion". Apart from the fact that common sense tells us that Buddhism has all the marks of a religion, and not a "philosophy", Buddhism is a religion for the simple reason that, unlike post-Renaissance "philosophies", it is not man-made, but has its origin in a divine revelation.

*

*   *

On receiving "enlightenment" (*bodhi*)—which amounted to the providential revelation of Buddhism—, Siddhārtha Gautama himself became the *Buddha* (the "Enlightened One"). He also enjoys other titles, such as, *Shākyamuni* ("Sage of the Shākya tribe"), *Shūnyamūrti* ("Manifestation of the Void" or "Exteriorization of the Inward"), and *Tathāgata* (the "Thus-Gone" or the "Fully-Arrived", i.e., the one who has himself accomplished, and now "incarnates" both the path and the Goal). The Buddha is also identified with *Mahākarunā*, the "Great Compassion".

The Buddha's life story, as outlined in the preceding pages, provides the framework for the central doctrine of the Buddhist religion, which the Buddha himself expressed in the following words: "I teach two things only, O disciples, suffering and release from suffering." His life story likewise provides the background for his doctrine of the "Middle Way" (Sanskrit: *madhyamā-pratipad*/Pali: *majjhima-pātipadā*), that is to say, the golden mean between asceticism and self-indulgence.

All the Buddha's essential teachings were given in his famous First Sermon, "the First Setting in Motion of the Wheel of the Law" (*Dharmachakra Pravatana*), and are enshrined in what are known as "The Four Noble Truths" and "The Eightfold Path".

Stone Wheel of the Law (*Dharmachakra*), Thailand, 7th-8th century

The Four Noble Truths

(1)   Suffering is universal.

(2)   The cause of suffering is craving or selfish desire (*trishnā*).

(3)   The cure for suffering is the elimination of craving.

(4)   The way to achieve the elimination of craving is to follow the Middle Way, the technique of which is described in the Eightfold Path.

The Eightfold Path

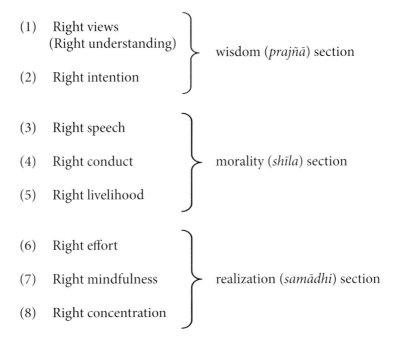

(1)   Right views
       (Right understanding)

(2)   Right intention

wisdom (*prajñā*) section

(3)   Right speech

(4)   Right conduct

(5)   Right livelihood

morality (*shīla*) section

(6)   Right effort

(7)   Right mindfulness

(8)   Right concentration

realization (*samādhi*) section

The Eightfold Path, with its three sections—"wisdom", "realization", and "morality"—thus exemplifies the three elements that are necessarily present in all religions: truth, spiritual way, and virtue.

Opposite page: *T'hanka* of Amogasiddhi Buddha, Central Tibet, c. 1200-1250

The element "conduct" in the morality section is made explicit in the practical code known as "The Five Precepts".

The Five Precepts

(1)   To abstain from the taking of life.

(2)   To abstain from the taking of what is not given.

(3)   To abstain from all illicit sexual activity.

(4)   To abstain from lying.

(5)   To abstain from intoxicants.

The doctrine of *karma* ("as a man sows, so shall he reap"), which is integral to Hinduism, is also present in Buddhism. For further discussion of *karma*, "karmic continuity", and the related doctrine of "reincarnation", see pp. 123-125.

*
* *

Like virtually every other religion, Buddhism sees mankind's history as a gradual, but accelerating, decline and envisages a forthcoming "end of the world", at which time the Buddha will return as Maitreya Buddha. A similar apocalyptic expectation exists in Hinduism in the form of the *Kalki-Avatāra*, and in Christianity and Islam in the form of the second coming of Christ.

*
* *

The Supreme Buddha (*Ādi-Buddha*) is said to have manifested Himself many times for the salvation of men. The *Buddhavamsa* (part of the *Khuddaka Nikāya*) lists ten manifestations of the *Ādi-Buddha* who "turned the Wheel of the Law in a deer sanctuary", eight of them preceding, and the tenth one (Maitreya) following, Gautama.

Standing Maitreya Buddha, Mongolia, early 18th century

These ten Buddhas are as follows (names in Pali, with Sanskrit in parentheses):

Dhammadassin

Siddhatta (Siddhārta)

Phussa

Vipassi (Vipashyin)

Sikhī (Shikin)

Kakusandha (Krakuchchanda)

Konāgamana (Kanakamuni)

Kassapa (Kāshyapa)

Gotama (Gautama) [the historical Buddha]

Metteyya (Maitreya) [the Buddha yet to come]

In Hinduism there are ten principal Incarnations (*Avatāra*s) of the God Vishnu. One may see a certain analogy between the Hindu and Buddhist series of ten Incarnations: in each series, the second-last personage is precisely Gautama Buddha, and the last is the "apocalyptic" Incarnation (Kalki or Maitreya respectively).

*

*   *

Following the example of the Buddha himself, the final goal of the Buddhist religion is the attainment of *Nirvāna* (the "Unconditioned" or "Divine State") from the starting-point of *samsāra* (the world)—in other words, the attainment of the Absolute from the starting-point of the relative. According to Buddhist doctrine, the principal hindrances to the realization of *Nirvāna* are the five "attributes of individuality" (*skandha*s). These are:

body (*rūpa*)

sensations (*vedanā*)

thoughts (*samjñā*)

desires (*samskāra*)

individual consciousness (*vijñāna*)

Opposite page: Gautama Buddha, Gupta Dynasty, Sārnāth, India

The five *skandha*s cause man to be susceptible to the three *klesha*s ("poisons" or "passions"), which are the very source of suffering (*duhkha*). These are:

ignorance or illusion (*moha*) — symbolized by a pig

greed or lust (*lobha*)   — symbolized by a cock

anger or pride (*dvesha*)   — symbolized by a snake

Illusion, lust, pride ("the world, the flesh, the devil"): these are the basic existential veils—or moral evils—to which all others can be reduced. The three symbolic animals are usually depicted swallowing each other, thus indicating the apparently hopeless predicament of those who are their dupes. The only release is in the merciful Buddha and in the Way he preached: the Four Noble Truths and the Eightfold Path. Thus may one transcend the *skandha*s (egoism) and overcome the *klesha*s (passions), and so escape the thralldom of *samsāra*. (For the *Mahāyāna* doctrine of the Bodhisattva and the "six virtues" or *pāramitā*s, see pp. 67-68 and 77.)

One who, through spiritual striving and the grace of the Buddha, attains the virtuality or actuality of the state of *Nirvāna* is known as an *arhat* or *arhant* (Sanskrit, "worthy one"), *arahat* (Pali), *lohan* (Chinese), or *rakan* (Japanese). These terms may be loosely translated as "saint". There are of course many degrees and modes of union with Ultimate Reality, and this is something of which Buddhism takes full account.

Nirvāna is as it were incarnated by the Buddha and this recalls the famous formula of St. Irenaeus—the definitive expression of the central role of the *Logos* in all spiritualities or mysticisms: "God became man, so that man might become God." In the case of Buddhism, this may be paraphrased as follows: *Nirvāna* became *samsāra*, so that *samsāra* might become *Nirvāna*.

This insight comes from Frithjof Schuon.[2] Elsewhere Schuon writes:

The invocation of the Buddha Amitābha is founded on a doctrine of redemption. Amitābha is the Light and the Life of

---

[2] See "The Perennial Philosophy", in *The Unanimous Tradition*, ed. Ranjit Fernando (Colombo: Sri Lanka Institute of Traditional Studies, 1991), pp. 22-23.

T'hanka of the Wheel of Life (*Bhavachakramudrā*),
with the three *klesha*s represented at the center, Tibet

the Buddha; in invoking Amitābha, the devotee enters into a golden halo of Mercy, he finds security in the blessed light of that Name; he withdraws into it with perfect surrender and also with perfect gratitude. The Name of Amitābha carries the devotee towards *Sukhāvatī* ("the Western Paradise").[3]

This is a reference to the Buddha's "Original Vow", which plays a central role in the Pure Land school (see pp. 79-80). The invocation of the Name of the Buddha corresponds to the invocatory spiritual methods of other religions, such as *japa-yoga* in Hinduism, the "Jesus Prayer" in Eastern Christianity, and *dhikr Allāh* (the "remembrance of God") in Islam. In Buddhism, the spiritual method of invocation or remembrance is known as *Buddhānusmriti* (Sanskrit), *nien-fo* (Chinese), and *nembutsu* (Japanese).

*

*   *

A well-known Buddhist doctrine is that of *anātmā* (Pali *anattā*), "non-self". This is said to be one of the "three conditions of existence" (*trilakshana*), namely:

impermanence (*anitya*)

suffering (*duhkha*)

non-self (*anātmā*)

It is important to understand that the doctrine of *anātmā* is not a denial of *Ātmā* (Self), as is commonly supposed. It simply tells us that creatures, to the extent that they are subject to the "three poisons" (illusion, lust, pride), are devoid of *Ātmā*. By the same token, those who, thanks to the revealed means of grace, have overcome illusion and passion—either really or virtually—have established (or are establishing) themselves in *Ātmā*. In Christian terms, "the kingdom of Heaven is within you". One must immediately add that to misunderstand this latter doctrine is the most lethal of spiritual poisons. To equate the unregenerate soul with the Divine is precisely the central flaw of "new age" ideology.

---

[3] *Stations of Wisdom* (London: John Murray, 1961) p. 144.

Opposite page: *Sukhāvatī*, the Western Paradise of Amitābha, Tibet, 18th century

In the famous incident when the Buddha met a group of people searching for a young woman (the symbol of *anātmā*, "non-self"), he said to them: "What think ye? Were it not better that ye sought the Self?" [*attānam gaveseyyātha*] (*Vinaya Pitaka*, i, 23). The Buddha made many references to the Self (*Ātmā*): "Make the Self your refuge" (*Samyutta Nikāya*, iii, 143). "Be such as have the Self as your refuge" (*Dīgha Nikāya*, ii, 101). "I have made the Self my refuge" (*Dīgha Nikāya*, ii, 120). The "Self", *Ātmā* (which in fact amounts to "God Immanent", the Nirvanic Reality), is as central to Buddhism as it is to Hinduism and other religions.

Again in the *Dīgha-Nikāya* (iii, 84), the *Tathāgata* is said to be "*Brahma*-become" and "*Dhamma*-become", which clearly underscores the equation of the *Tathāgata* (the Buddha) with *Brahma* (the Supreme Divinity), *Dhamma* (the Law or Norm)—as well as with *Ātmā* (the Self). (See also *Samyutta-Nikāya*, iii, 120, quoted on the next page.)

There is a parallel to the Buddhist doctrine of "non-self" (*anattā*) in the Judeo-Christian Scripture. Only God can say: "I am that I am". Only *Ātmā* is fully and truly real. It is recorded that Christ said to St. Catherine of Siena in a vision: "Thou art she who is not; I am He who is." St. Catherine herself said: "I find no more *me*; there is no longer any other *I* but God." St. Paul proclaimed the same truth, when he said: "Not I, but Christ in me." The Christian teaching, like the Buddhist, makes clear the merely relative reality of all that is not Absolute, and is a necessary doctrinal prelude to spiritual endeavor.

In Islam also there is a parallel, and this is in the declaration of faith: "there is no god but God". Some of the Islamic mystics, or Sufis, interpret this basic dogma in a manner that is in complete accord with Buddhist doctrine, namely, "there is no reality but the one Reality", which amounts to saying "there is no self but the Self". They also speak of the need for "extinction" (*fanā'*) of the lower soul (*nafs*) and of "permanence" (*baqā'*) in God. Buddhist spiritual teaching lays the emphasis on the emptiness (*anattā*) of the lower soul; only the *arhant* (the saint who has overcome *samsāra* and achieved *Nirvāna*) is fully "awakened", fully "*Dhamma*-become".

Paraphrasing Molière, we can say that there is emptiness and emptiness, as well as fullness and fullness: there is the vain fullness of the world (*samsāra*) and the sacred Emptiness of the Void (*Shūnyatā*); at the same time there is the vain emptiness of the unregenerate soul (*anattā*) and the sacred Fullness of the Self (*Ātmā*).

Vajradhara Buddha, Mongolia, 17th century

Just as Christianity has its roots, not in creation but in the Creator, so Buddhism has its roots, not in *samsāra* (the "illusory", the deceptive) but in *Nirvāna* (the Real, the True), variously referred to, in different contexts, as *Dharma* ("Law", "Norm", "Truth"), *Bodhi* ("Enlightenment", "Knowledge"), and *Ātmā* ("Self"). Buddhism's message for suffering man is that herein alone lies "release from suffering" or, as Christianity would say, salvation.

Let it be said here that metaphysics is *not* absent from Buddhism; Buddhism is not merely a methodology, as is sometimes alleged. The efficacy of its method is based on the truth of its doctrine. Anything else would be inconceivable.

*
* *

As mentioned on p. 23, Buddhism, like Hinduism and Christianity, is "incarnationist" and "iconodulic". Buddha not only teaches doctrine— "turns the Wheel (*chakra*) of the Law (*dharma*)"—but actually incarnates *Nirvāna*. The image of the Buddha—of supernatural origin—is of profound sacramental importance in Buddhist spirituality. In this connection, it is said: "The Buddha also teaches by means of his superhuman beauty."

*
* *

In Christianity, much importance is given to the doctrine of the *Logos*. In fact, the doctrine of the *Logos* (whatever name it be given) is central to every religion, for the *Logos* is the indispensable link between man and God.

Within each religion, the Founder is the personification of the *Logos*, and his role as such is always made explicit. Christ said: "No man cometh to the Father but by me." Mohammed said: "No one will meet God who has not first met His Prophet", and also: "He that hath seen me (the Prophet), hath seen the Truth (God)." In Buddhism, it is strikingly similar: the Buddha said: "He who sees the *Dhamma* sees me, and he who sees me sees the *Dhamma*" (*Samyutta-Nikāya*, iii, 120).

It is precisely this identification with the *Logos* which enables and requires each Founder (Prophet or *Avatāra*) to speak in such absolute terms. Were it not so, there would be no question of a religion, nor would there be any possibility of salvation.

Opposite page: Phra Buddha Jinnarat of Pitsanulok, Thailand, 15th century

The most elementary religious viewpoint envisages two fundamental realities, namely God and man or Creator and created. In Buddhism, the corresponding pair would be *Nirvāna* and *samsāra*. Within
each of these two realities, however, a distinction can be made. As regards man, it is clear that man consists of body and soul (pertaining
respectively to the corporeal realm and the subtle or psychic realm). As
regards God (or the Nirvanic Reality), the distinction to be made, according to the metaphysicians and mystical theologians of all the great
religions, is as follows:

(1)   The Divine Essence (the level of "Beyond-Being")
      —the "Supra-Personal" God.

(2)   God as Creator, Sustainer, and Judge (the level of "Being")
      —the "Personal" God.

Thus we reach four levels of reality: two human and two divine.
Most importantly, there is, between the two Divine and the two purely
human levels, the level of what the Ancient and Medieval philosophers
and theologians called the Spirit (*Spiritus* or *Pneuma*) or Intellect
(*Intellectus* or *Nous*). The Spirit or Intellect (in Sanskrit, *Buddhi*), although "created", is supra-formal and "universal". It is directly touched
by the "Nirvanic" or the Divine. The soul, on the other hand, is formal
and "individual". Pertaining to the Intellect are such things as our conscience and our sense of justice. Above all, the Intellect is the faculty
which enables man to conceive the Absolute, and to know the Truth.
It is the source of his capacity for objectivity, of his ability—in contradistinction from the animals—to free himself from imprisonment in
subjectivity. It is the very definition of the human state.
    The term "Intellect" must not be confused with "mind" (faculty of
discursive reason) which, along with imagination, memory, sentiment,
and will, is one of the contents of the soul (*anima* or *psyche*).
    The Spirit or Intellect belongs to the "angelic" realm, the realm of
the Platonic archetypes. It supplies the only "archetypal" or objective
element in the constitution of man. The Intellect is thus the "measure"
of the soul; the soul can never be the "measure" of the Intellect. Spirit
and Intellect are the two sides of the same coin, the latter pertaining to
Truth (or doctrine) and the former to Being (or realization).

Rock-cut statue of the Buddha,
Gal Vihara, Polonnaruwa, Sri Lanka, 11th century

It is perhaps worth mentioning in passing that the fatal error of the modern psychologists (notably Jung) is their hopeless confusion of Spirit and soul, which in practice amounts to the "abolition" of Spirit. This is the "abolition" of the Absolute—and the objective—with a vengeance, and it has had disastrous consequences for religion and spirituality.

Without the concept—and the reality—of the Spirit or Intellect, no contact whatsoever between God and man would be possible. This indeed seems to be the position of the Deists. The Spirit or Intellect in fact corresponds to the *created Logos*, while God as "Being" is the *uncreated Logos*. It is thus that the *Logos*, with its two "Faces" (created and uncreated), constitutes the "bridge" between man and God.

The uncreated *Logos* is the prefiguration of the relative in the Absolute (this is God as Creator) and the created *Logos* is the reflection of the Absolute in the relative (this is, on the one hand, Truth and Virtue, Symbol and Sacrament; and, on the other, *Avatāra*, *Tathāgata*, Redeemer, or Prophet).

In Buddhism, these five levels of reality appear in the form of the three "hypostases" or "bodies" (*trikāya*) of the Buddha. These are as follows:

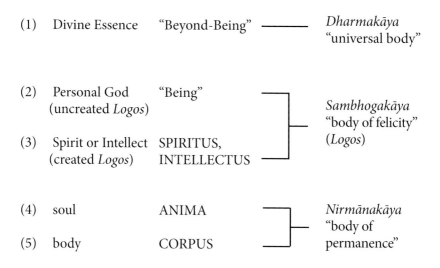

(1)	Divine Essence	"Beyond-Being"	*Dharmakāya* "universal body"
(2)	Personal God (uncreated *Logos*)	"Being"	*Sambhogakāya* "body of felicity" (*Logos*)
(3)	Spirit or Intellect (created *Logos*)	SPIRITUS, INTELLECTUS	
(4)	soul	ANIMA	*Nirmānakāya* "body of
(5)	body	CORPUS	permanence"

Level (1), "Beyond-Being" or the Divine Essence, is the Absolute. Level (2), "Being" or the Personal God, is the first autodetermination of the Absolute and the beginning of relativity. In Hindu terms, this is the distinction between *Ātmā* and *Māyā*. Levels (3), (4), and (5) taken together constitute creation, existence, or manifestation.

In the metaphysical terminology of René Guénon, one can say that, macrocosmically, level (3) is "supra-formal manifestation" (the Paradisal or angelic realm). Levels (2) and (3) taken together have been called "higher *Māyā*". There is an intimation of "higher *Māyā*" in the world seen as theophany.

Macrocosmically, levels (4) and (5) taken together constitute "formal manifestation" (the "world" or *samsāra*). This is "lower *māyā*"— the world as exile and separation from God.

Although, metaphysically, "lower *māyā*" (*samsāra*) is illusion, at the human or moral level, it is the source of temptation, and is powerfully ensnaring; it is notoriously unwilling to release those whom it holds in thrall. On the contrary, "higher *Māyā*"—mediated and made accessible by divine revelation, as well as by inspiration and intellection—is liberating and saving. In Christian terminology, it is the difference between Eve and Mary. In Buddhism, it is suffering and release from suffering.

The Founders of the great religions are incarnations of the *Logos*— levels (2) and (3).[4]

Of what use are words of wisdom to a man who is unwise?
Of what use is a lamp to a man who is blind?

Dhammapada

---

[4] For a very clear explanation, see Frithjof Schuon, *Form and Substance in the Religions*, chap. 5, "The Five Divine Presences" (Bloomington IN: World Wisdom, 2002).

Map of the Buddhist World
(circa 1900)

The map below indicates virtually all of the countries which comprise the Buddhist area of the world

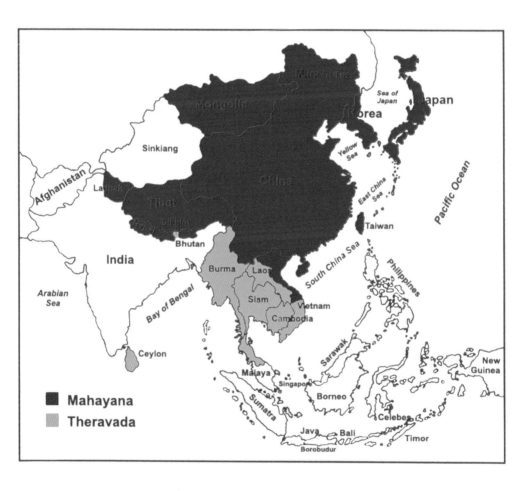

(9) The Two Schools and the Two Cultural Forms

In the face of a reformed and reviving Hinduism and the irruption and expansion of Islam, Buddhism began to decline in India in the seventh century A.D. and by the thirteenth century had become virtually extinct in the land of its birth. It spread, however, to almost all of Eastern Asia.

A few centuries after its birth, Buddhism began to crystallize into two great schools, the Southern and the Northern. The Northern school or *Mahāyāna* ("Great" or "Broad" Way), which began to take form towards the beginning of the Christian era, called everything that came before it *Hīnayāna* ("Small" or "Narrow" Way). Although the term *Hīnayāna* has been applied diminishingly, it refers in a positive sense to the original monastic or ascetic Way, and is not in itself disparaging. The *Hīnayāna* school had many branches or sects, including *Theravāda*, *Mahāsānghika*, *Vātsīputrīya*, and *Sarvāstivāda*. Of these only *Theravāda* (the "Doctrine of the Elders") survives. The Southern school, *Hīnayāna* (in fact *Theravāda*), comprises Ceylon (Sri Lanka), Burma, Siam (Thailand), Cambodia, and Laos. The Northern school *Mahāyāna*, comprises China, Tibet, Ladhak, Nepal, Bhutan, Mongolia, Japan, Korea, and Vietnam.

The *Mahāyāna* and *Hīnayāna* art styles—as well as the two cultures in general—have distinctive and recognizable "flavors". In this connection, Frithjof Schuon has alluded to a certain ethnic and spiritual reciprocity by observing that, in the *Mahāyāna* countries, Buddhism has been absorbed by the "Yellow" genius, whereas in the *Hīnayāna* countries the "Yellow" genius has been absorbed by Buddhism. Metaphorically speaking, the *Mahāyāna* world is India become "Yellow", whereas *Hīnayāna* Buddhists (e.g. the Theravādins of Indo-China) are "Yellow" people who have, as it were, become Indian.[1]

It may be of interest to note in passing that the only Buddhist community in Europe are the Kalmuks, a Mongol people who, in the seventeenth century, migrated westward from Central Asia to Russia—to the region now known as Kalmykia, on the north-western shores of the Caspian Sea between the Muslim regions of Astrakhan and Dagestan.

Theravāda Buddhism is a continuation of original Buddhism, as regards its form if not as regards its whole content. *Mahāyāna* Bud-

[1] See Frithjof Schuon, *Castes and Races* (London: Perennial Books, 1982), p. 43, note 31.

dhism also derives from original Buddhism, but some of its charac-teristic manifestations spring from a later inspiration. In some of its aspects an influence from Hinduism is discernible.

The Scriptures of original Buddhism are recorded in Pali (a de-rivative of Sanskrit), and this language remains the liturgical medium of the Southern (or *Theravāda*) school. The original scriptural and li-turgical language of the Northern (or *Mahāyāna*) school is Sanskrit, but, in view of the geographical extension of *Mahāyāna*, this is supple-mented by Tibetan, Chinese, and Japanese. For more on the Scriptures, see pp. 16-17.[2]

Mahāyāna Buddhism, the second "Setting in Motion of the Wheel of the Law" (*Dharmachakra-Pravatana*), is characterized above all by the doctrine and cult of the Bodhisattva (see pp. 67-70 and 77). Fur-thermore, in *Mahāyāna* countries, Buddhism generally finds itself in a state of co-existence or symbiosis with one or more indigenous reli-gions. In China, Buddhism co-exists with the "esoteric" and spiritual (and yet, at the same time, popular) doctrine and traditions of Taoism, and also with the "exoteric" and social (and yet, at the same time, aris-tocratic) doctrine and traditions of Confucianism. In Japan, Buddhism co-exists with Shintoism; in Tibet, it co-exists with Bön.

As can be seen from the table on page 10, Taoism, Confucianism, Shinto, and Bön are branches of Hyperborean shamanism. Unlike the various Aryan and Semitic religions, shamanisms are not "denomina-tional" and exclusive. Thus, while it is impossible to be a member of two different "denominational" religions at the same time, it is per-fectly possible to be a member of a shamanistic and a denominational religion at the same time. One sees this, precisely, in the case of the Chinese, Japanese, and Tibetans, and also in the case of many Red In-dians, who see nothing untoward in belonging to a Christian denomi-nation while, at the same time, believing in and practicing the religion of the Sun Dance and the Sacred Pipe.

Within *Mahāyāna* Buddhism there are two distinct perspectives, one "sapiential" and the other "devotional". These have crystallized re-spectively into *Dhyāna*, *Ch'an*, or Zen Buddhism on the one hand, and

---

[2] With but few exceptions, the original Buddhist terms cited in this book are given in their Sanskrit form. Pali versions of some of these terms are as follows: *Nibbana* (for *Nirvāna*), *Dhamma* (for *Dharma*), *Attā* (for *Ātmā*), *Sutta* (for *Sūtra*), *Siddhatta* (for *Siddhārtha*), *Gotama* (for *Gautama*), *Metteyya* (for *Maitreya*), *Theravāda* (for *Sthaviravāda*).

Sukhāvatī, Ching-t'u-tsung, or *Jōdo* ("Pure Land") Buddhism (sometimes known as Amida Buddhism) on the other. (In each case the names are given successively in Sanskrit, Chinese, and Japanese.) As religious forms, these branches represent two extreme positions, but each, nevertheless, is orthodox, in that it is a possible and legitimate development of the original Buddhist revelation.

The distinction "sapiential"/"devotional", although valid, is not absolute. Thus *Jōdo* (or "Pure Land"), though providentially the representative of devotion (*bhakti* in Hindu terminology), possesses in its scriptures the fundamental elements of sapiential metaphysics. Likewise, the more overtly intellectual Zen sects have also, throughout their long history, included intensely devotional currents.

In Zen, the point of view is that of "own-power" (Japanese: *jiriki*), whereas in *Jōdo*, the point of view is that of "power of the Other" (Japanese: *tariki*). One can explain this difference in Western terms by saying that Zen is based on the view that man was created in the image of God, and relates to the concept of "God Immanent", whereas, *Jōdo* is based on the view that man is but a fallen creature in need of mercy, and relates to the concept of "God Transcendent". It is as if, in Christianity, two distinct monastic or spiritual traditions had arisen, one based on the text "The Kingdom of God is within you" (Luke 17:21), and the other on the text "Whosoever shall call upon the Name of the Lord shall be saved" (Romans 10:13). For fuller details on the Pure Land school, see pp. 79-80.

The "sapiential" perspective within *Mahāyāna* Buddhism is also manifested in *Vajrayāna* (the "Diamond Vehicle"), which, in view of its importance, is called the "Third School" or the third "Setting in Motion of the Wheel of the Law". *Vajrayāna* is the Buddhist form of *tantra*, a religious perspective and practice well-known in Shivaite Hinduism, and based on the masculine and feminine principles *purusha* and *prakriti*. The Buddhist form of *tantra* is sometimes referred to as the "marriage" of *upāya* and *prajñā*. It should be noted that, in this pair of celestial principles, it is *upāya* ("formal doctrine and method") which is masculine and *prajñā* ("formless wisdom") which is feminine. For fuller details on the Buddhist form of *tantra* see pp. 93-97.

Yet another school which would fall into the "sapiential" category is *Avatamsaka* or *Hua-yen* ("Flower Garland"), one of the most important schools in China, and occurring in Japan as *Kegon*. For fuller details on the Chinese and Japanese schools, see pp. 101-102 and 116-117.

U Thong bronze Buddha, Thailand, 14th-15th century

Neither the slothful, nor the fool, nor the undiscerning can reach Nirvana.

Iti-vuttaka

Bodhisattva Avalokiteshvara, Nepal, c. 12th century

It is a terrible fact that devils always get in the way of those who are striving for Buddhahood.

Hōnen

The Two Schools or the Two Cultural Forms

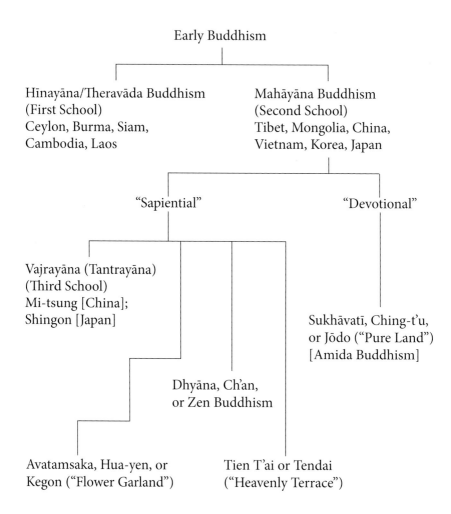

The Main Developmental Phases[1]

I. Hīnayāna/Early Buddhism
    ("Narrow Way")

II. Hīnayāna/Theravāda Buddhism
    (continuation of the foregoing,
    as regards its form, if not as
    regards its whole content)

III. Mahāyāna Buddhism
    ("Broad Way")

"Sapiential" — Vajrayāna
Hua-yen
Zen
Tien T'ai

"Devotional" — Amidism

---

[1] See Frithjof Schuon, *Treasures of Buddhism* (Bloomington IN: World Wisdom, 1993), pp. 34, 109-111, 136-137.

White Tārā as the personification of
Supreme Wisdom (*Prajñāpāramitā*), Java, c. 1300

(10) The Twenty-Eight Indian Patriarchs of Dhyana, Ch'an, or Zen Buddhism

Twenty-eight Indian patriarchs after the Buddha who are recognized by the *Dhyāna, Ch'an,* or Zen sect as having transmitted the "Seal of Spirit" down to Bodhidharma, who went to China in 520 A.D. and there became the first Chinese patriarch of *Ch'an.*

(1) Kāshyapa*	(11) Punyayasha	(20) Shayata
(2) Ānanda*	(12) Ashvaghosha	(21) Vasubandhu*
(3) Shānavāsin	(13) Kapimala	(22) Manorata
(4) Upagupta	(14) Nāgārjuna*	(23) Haklena
(5) Dhītak	(15) Kānadeva	(24) Simha
(6) Mishaka	(16) Rāhulabhadra	(25) Bashashita
(7) Vasumitra	(17) Samghanandi	(26) Punyamitra
(8) Buddhanandi	(18) Samghayathata	(27) Prajñādhāra*
(9) Buddhamitra	(19) Kumāralāta	(28) Bodhidharma*
(10) Pārshva		

* See index for further references to these personages

How can there be laughter, how can there be pleasure, when the whole world is burning? When ye are in deep darkness, will ye not ask for a lamp?

Dhammapada, 146

Bodhidharma (*seated*) and Hui-k'o, hanging scroll, Muromachi period, Japan, 1496

Thou shalt not let thy senses make a playground of thy mind.
The Voice of Silence

(11) The Six Chinese Patriarchs of Dhyana, Ch'an, or Zen Buddhism

The Japanese names are given within square brackets.

(1) Tamo (Bodhidharma*)	[Daruma]	(c. 470-543)
(2) Hui-k'o	[Eka]	(487-593)
(3) Seng ts'an	[Sōsan]	(d. 608?)
(4) Tao-hsin	[Dōshin]	(580-651)
(5) Hung-jen	[Gunin]	(601-674)
(6) Hui-neng	[Enō]	(638-713)

* See index for further references to these personages

When the finger points at the moon, the foolish man looks at the finger.

Zen saying

Hōnen at the Halo Bridge

It is told that once Ānanda, the beloved disciple of the Buddha, saluted his master and said: "Half of the holy life, O master, is friendship with the beautiful, association with the beautiful, communion with the beautiful."

"Say not so, Ānanda, say not so!" the master replied. "It is not half the holy life, it is the whole of the holy life."

                                   Samyutta-Nikāya

(12) The Seven Patriarchs of the Pure Land School of Mahayana Buddhism

The doctrine and practice of the Pure Land school of *Mahāyāna* Buddhism (Sanskrit *Sukhāvatī*; Chinese *Ching-t'u*; Japanese *Jōdo*) are founded on the Buddha's "Original Vow". Essentially it is a question of total reliance on the saving power of the Name of the Buddha Amitābha (Amida). See pp. 79-80.

The Japanese names of the Chinese patriarchs are given within square brackets.

Nāgārjuna*	(2nd century A.D.)	Indian
Vasubandhu*	(4th century A.D.)	
T'an-Luan [Donran]	(476-542 A.D.)	Chinese
T'ao-Ch'o* [Doshaku]	(561-644 A.D.)	
Shan-Tao [Zendo]	(613-681 A.D.)	
Genshin	(942-1017 A.D.)	Japanese
Hōnen*	(1133-1212 A.D.)	

Other eminent Japanese representatives of the *Jōdo* school—not however counted amongst the patriarchs—were Kūya (903-972) and Ryōnin (1072-1132). A prominent disciple of Hōnen was Shōnin Shinran* (1173-1262), founder of the *Jōdo-shin* school.

* See index for further references to these personages

Whoever has faith in Me and love for Me is assured of rebirth in Heaven.
                                    The Buddha (*Majjhima-Nikāya*, i,142)

Amida Buddha, Japan, 1202-1208

Fools of poor understanding have themselves for their greatest enemies, for they do evil deeds which bear bitter fruits.
Dhammapada, 66

(13) Buddhas and Bodhisattvas

Etymologically, *buddha* means "enlightened", and *bodhisattva* means "one whose nature is enlightenment". In *Mahāyāna* Buddhism, the term *bodhisattva* has been traditionally understood to mean an "aspirant for Buddhahood"—one who seeks Buddhahood through the transcending of the five "attributes of individuality" (*skandha*s) and the acquiring of the six virtues (*pāramitā*s). (See pp. 39 and 77 respectively.)

The Bodhisattva is also said to be "one who renounces final entry into *Nirvāna* until all beings are saved", and in this connection, the element compassion (*karunā*) is foremost. This formulation is no doubt operative in intention, but it is nevertheless paradoxical in form, as it can scarcely be that a Bodhisattva needs to stop short of *Nirvāna* in order to be able to save others.

Let us observe parenthetically that the *Dhammapada* (159 and 166) makes it clear that man's first duty is to save his soul. This is the very opposite of being "selfish"! To escape from the clutches of *samsāra* is the greatest possible service that one can render to others. This is true in the case of ordinary morality as well as in the case of contemplative monasticism: the *Dhammapada* (54) states: "The perfume of virtue travels against the wind and reaches unto the ends of the earth."

The merciful function envisaged by the *Mahāyāna* doctrine is the salvation of believers by the bestowal upon them of the merit of the Bodhisattva. In other words, it means the redemption of creatures, hopelessly afflicted with ignorance and suffering, by the saving power of Another. This is precisely the role of the Bodhisattva. (See "The Bodhisattva's Undertaking" on p. 70 and "Dharmākara's Vow" on p. 79.)

The saving compassion of the Bodhisattva is contrasted with the condition of the *pratyeka-buddha*, who is a "solitary" who achieves enlightenment without possessing the function or mission of communicating it to others. On the contrary, the Bodhisattva possesses the state of the *samyaksam-buddha*, whose providentially ordained cosmic wisdom endows him with the ability—and the mission—to transmit the saving message and the saving grace to the world.

Mahāyāna Buddhism teaches that there are two kinds of Bodhisattvas: terrestrial and celestial. Terrestrial Bodhisattvas are characterized by their compassion, manifested chiefly by their thrust towards salvation or enlightenment (for themselves and others). Celestial Bodhisattvas have actualized the six *pāramitā*s, possess buddhahood, and, while not being subject to *samsāra*, are nevertheless present within it for the salvation of men. In the *Mahāyāna* perspective, compassion is seen as a dimension of knowledge, and the Bodhisattva is the very incarnation of this.

Amongst the many celestial Bodhisattvas are Avalokiteshvara (the Bodhisattva of Mercy), Mahāsthāmaprāpta (the one who awakens men to the need for salvation), Mañjushrī (the Bodhisattva of Wisdom), Kshitigarbha—in Japan Jizō—(the savior from hell and the protector of children and travelers), and Achala Vidyārāja—in Japan Fudō—(the opponent of the world's inequities, stupor, and indifference to truth).

The feminine aspect of Avalokiteshvara, known in China as Kwan-Yin and in Japan as Kwannon, is particularly venerated in these two countries. Kwan-Yin is often assimilated to Tārā, who is venerated in Tibet as the Consort of Avalokiteshvara (see p. 89).

A Buddha can be said to be one who has come from Heaven to earth in order to reveal the path that leads from earth to Heaven (i.e. the achieving of *Nirvāna* from the starting-point of *samsāra*—the achieving of the Absolute from the starting-point of the relative). A Bodhisattva, for his part, is a helping, compassionate, salvific, and Nirvanic presence within *samsāra* itself. His role may be compared to the Christian doctrine of the Holy Spirit as an ever-present Helper in this world.

In a certain sense, it could be said that the grace of the Buddha is static or intrinsic, and the grace of the Bodhisattva dynamic or extrinsic. Frithjof Schuon has given a metaphysical exposition of the relationship of the Buddha and the Bodhisattva as follows: The three fundamental attributes of the Divine Nature—the three fundamental hypostases of Unity—are Absoluity, Infinity, and Perfection. These may be symbolized geometrically as Center, Radii, and Circumference. In Christian terms, the Father is the Absolute (the Center), the Holy Spirit is the Infinite (the Radii), and the Son is the Perfect (the Circumference—the Incarnation of God in the world). In Buddhist terms, *Nirvāna* is the Absolute (the Center), the Bodhisattva is the Infinite (the Radii), and the Buddha is the Perfect (the Circumference—in this case, the presence of *Nirvāna* in *samsāra*). In both cases, the Infinite is the Radii emerging from the Center and returning to it. This symbolical way of looking at things enables us to see, firstly, the respective functions of the Buddha and the Bodhisattva, and also the analogy between the functions of the Holy Spirit and the Bodhisattva.[1]

---

[1] See Frithjof Schuon, "Hypostatic Dimensions of Unity", in *Sufism: Veil and Quintessence* (Bloomington, IN: World Wisdom, 2006), and "The Mystery of the Bodhisattva", in *Treasures of Buddhism*; Titus Burckhardt, "The Image of the Buddha", in *Sacred Art in East and West*; Peter Masefield, *Divine Revelation in Pali Buddhism*; and Marco Pallis, "Is There Room for Grace in Buddhism?", in *A Buddhist Spectrum* (Bloomington, IN: World Wisdom, 2003).

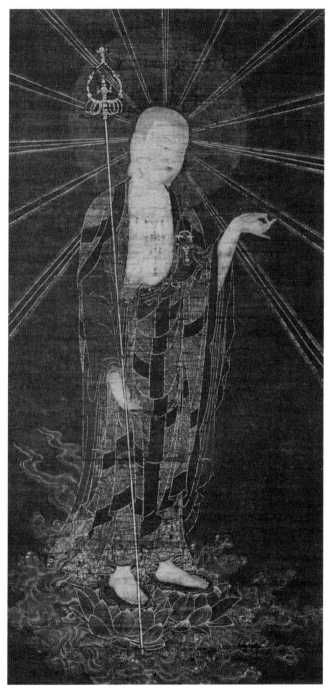

Bodhisattva Kshitigarbha, Kamakura period, Japan

The Bodhisattva's Undertaking

I take upon myself . . . the deeds of all beings, even those in the hells, in the other worlds, and in the realms of punishment. . . . I take their suffering upon me, . . . I bear it, I do not draw back from it, I do not tremble at it, I have no fear of it, . . . I do not lose heart. . . . I must bear the burden of all beings, for I have vowed to save all things living, to bring them safe through the forest of birth, age, disease, birth, and re-birth. I think not of my own salvation, but strive to bestow on all beings the royalty of supreme wisdom. So I take upon myself all the sorrows of all beings. I resolve to bear every torment in every purgatory of the universe. For it is better that I alone should suffer than that the multitude of living beings should suffer. I give myself in exchange. I redeem the universe from the forest of purgatory, from the womb of flesh, from the realm of death. I agree to suffer as a ransom for all beings, and for the sake of all beings. Truly I will not abandon them. For I have resolved to gain supreme wisdom for the sake of all.

Vajradhvaja Sūtra

Above: Sanjūsangendō Temple, Kyoto, Japan, 1226.
The hall contains 1,000 different images of the Bodhisattva Kwannon;
Right: The central statue of Bodhisattva Kwannon, Sanjūsangendō Temple, Kyoto;
Following pages: White Tārā (*left*) and Mahāvairochana (*right*), the Supreme
Feminine and Masculine Principles, Mongolia, 17th century

Buddhas and Bodhisattvas: Some Correspondences

Buddha or Bodhisattva	Description or Name	Correspondence	Spatial Symbol
Ādi-Buddha (*Vajradhara, Mahāvairochana*)	Supreme Masculine Principle	Essence, *Prajñāpāramitā*, Supreme Gnosis	zenith
Tārā	Supreme Feminine Principle ("Mother of all Buddhas and Bodhisattvas")	Substance, *Prajñāpāramitā*, Supreme Gnosis	nadir
Dhyāni-Buddhas (*Jinas*)	Vairochana ["The Great Illuminator"]	ether	center
	Amogasiddhi ["Dispassion", "Charity"]	earth	N
	Akshobya ["The Immovable One"]	air	E
	Amitābha ["Immeasurable Light"]	water	W
	Ratnasambhava ["Equanimity", "Humility"]	fire	S
Bodhisattvas	Maitreya ["The One still to come"]	—	NE
	Samantabhadra ["Life", "Action"]	—	NW
	Mañjushrī ["Wisdom"]	—	SW
	Avalokiteshvara ["Mercy", "Compassion"]	—	SE

Buddhas and Bodhisattvas: Names in Different Languages

Buddha or Bodhisattva	Pali	Sanskrit	Tibetan	Chinese	Japanese	*Lama Tulku* in Tibet (see p. 99)
The Buddha who presides over the "Western Paradise"	—	Amitābha	Opagmed	O-mi-tò Fu'	Amida	Panchen Lama
The Bodhisattva of Mercy	—	Avalokiteshvara	Chenrezig	Kwan-Yin	Kwannon	Dalai Lama
The Bodhisattva of Wisdom	—	Mañjushrī	Jambaiyang	Wen-shu	Monju	—
The Buddha to come	Metteyya	Maitreya	Chamba	Mi-lo Fu	Miroku	—

Avalokiteshvara, the Bodhisattva of Mercy,
Bihar, India, 10th century

*Just as the ocean has only one flavor, the flavor of salt, so my
doctrine has only one flavor, the flavor of release from sorrow.*
The Buddha (*Vinaya Pitaka*, i, 239)

(14) The Six Paramitas
("Virtues of the Bodhisattva")

Pāramitā means literally "that which has reached the other shore" (see
p. 134). In *Mahāyāna* Buddhism, it is taught that the six *pāramitā*s are
the virtues of the Bodhisattva. These are: *dāna* ("charity"), *shīla* ("ab-
stention"), *kshānti* ("patience"), *vīrya* ("virility"), *dhyāna* ("contempla-
tion"), and *prajñā* ("wisdom").

Some symbolic correspondences with the directions of space, the
elements, and the *Dhyāni-Buddha*s are shown below.[1]

1	2
shīla ("abstention")	*vīrya* ("virility")
N — earth	E — air
Amogasiddhi	Akshobya

3	4
kshānti ("patience")	*dāna* ("charity")
W — water	S — fire
Amitābha	Ratnasambhava

5	6
dhyāna ("contemplation", "discernment")	*prajñā* ("wisdom", "union")
ZENITH — ether	NADIR — Void (*Shūnyatā*)
Vairochana	Vajradhara (Mahāvairochana)

---

[1] See the chapter on the "Synthesis of the *Pāramitā*s" in Frithjof Schuon, *Treasures of Buddhism*, pp. 126-127.

Amida Buddha flanked by Dai-Seishi and Kwannon, Kyoto, Japan, 1148

*Even as one who desires to reach a longed-for city requires eyes
to see the way and feet to traverse it, so also the one who desires
to reach the City of* Nirvāna *requires the eyes of Doctrine and
the feet of Method.*

Prajñā-Pāramitā-Sūtra

(15) The Original Vow and the Pure Land School

The Buddha made forty-eight vows (*pranidhānas*), of which the eighteenth, called by Hōnen "the king of the vows", is known as the "Original Vow":

> When I have attained the state of Buddha ("Enlightened"), if the beings in the ten regions (of the universe), who have believed in Me with a calm mind, have desired to be born again in my Country, and have remembered (thought on) Me, be it only ten times, are not reborn there, may I not obtain Perfect Knowledge. Excepted are only those who have committed the five mortal sins and have blasphemed the Good Law. (*Sukhāvatī-Vyūha-Sūtra*, major, 8:18)

In the *Amitāyur-Dhyāna-Sūtra*, the Buddha reiterates this promise by telling the story of "Dharmākara's Vow": a Bodhisattva called Dharmākara, when on the threshold of *Nirvāna*, made a vow not to enter therein if, once he had become Buddha ("Enlightened"), he were unable to offer a Paradise of Purity to all who pronounced his Name—henceforth nirvanic or divine—with unmixed faith and in the conviction of being incapable of saving themselves by their own merits. Having achieved Buddhahood under the Name of Amitābha or Amitāyus (the two go together), the celestial Personage keeps his word: by the power of his Name he delivers a multitude of believers. The Buddha Shākyamuni participates in this work by retelling Dharmākara's story and thus bringing it to the attention of mankind. The Paradise to be attained is the "Pure Land" (*Sukhāvatī*, literally "land of bliss") or the "Western Paradise" over which Amitābha (Japanese Amida) reigns.

Amitābha = infinite light — equated with *prajñā* (wisdom)
Amitāyus = infinite life — equated with *karunā* (compassion)

Reference was made on pp. 40-43 to the presence, in all the great religions, of the spiritual method that is based on the invocation of a revealed Divine Name: *japa-yoga* in Hinduism, the "Jesus Prayer" in Eastern Christianity, and *dhikr Allāh* (the "remembrance of God") in Islam. In Buddhism this invocatory method is known as the "remembrance of the Buddha": *Buddhānusmriti* (Sanskrit), *nien-fo* (Chinese), and *nembutsu* (Japanese).

This "remembrance" or "invocation" is the central spiritual practice of the Pure Land School of Buddhism (Sanskrit *Sukhāvatī*, Chinese *Ching-t'u*, Japanese *Jōdo*), the scriptural basis of which is the Buddha's "Original Vow". The invocatory formula (*mantra*) of the "Pure Land" school is:

Namo 'mitābhaya Buddhāya (Sanskrit)

Na-mu O-mit'o Fu' (Chinese)

Namu Amida Butsu (Japanese)

The literal meaning of this invocation or *mantra* is: "I take refuge in the Buddha of Infinite Light and Infinite Life." (For the original Sanskrit and Chinese scripts, see pp. 106-107.) Its solemn and prayerful repetition is a "sacrament", a means of grace, at the heart of which lies an unquestioning faith in the saving power of the revealed Name.

The Hindus emphasize the particular appositeness and efficacy of *japa-yoga* in the context of mankind's spiritual weakness in these latter days of decadence (the *Kali-Yuga*). Analogously, the Pure Land school of Buddhism emphasizes the appositeness and efficacy of the doctrine and practice of *nembutsu* in the *mappō*, "the decadent age of the *Dharma*".

This method of salvation through the continual invocation of a revealed Name of the Divinity (or the Absolute) is an example of what St. Paul called "prayer without ceasing". Its particularity lies in the fact that it is accessible to all (i.e. to sinners), on the one condition that they have a total trust in the Divine Mercy—or, in this case, in the Buddheic Grace. Unlike the spiritual methods of earlier ages, this spiritual method is (apparently and outwardly) "easy"; that is to say, it does not require *a priori* severe fasting, prolonged liturgies, arduous pilgrimages, etc. It is based exclusively on faith and prayer—these being implicitly and logically accompanied by "good works". From another point of view, however, this method is far from easy, as it demands from the one following it a commitment that is both enduring and profound.[1]

---

[1] See *Treasures of Buddhism* by Frithjof Schuon, pp. 141-142 (note 4) and pp. 154-158.

Greeting picture of Amida Buddha and twenty-five bodhisattvas, Kongobu-ji, Japan

Whatever son or daughter of a family shall hear the Name of the Blessed Amitāyus, the Tathāgata, *and having heard it shall keep it in their mind . . . when that son or daughter of a family comes to die, then Amitāyus, the* Tathāgata, *will stand before them at the hour of death, and they will depart this life with tranquil minds; they will be reborn in Paradise.*

Sukhāvatī-Vyūha-Sūtra, 10

Temple of the Sacred Tooth Relic of the Buddha, Kandy, Sri Lanka

If a foolish man spends the whole of his life with a wise man, he never knows the path of wisdom as the spoon never knows the taste of soup. If a sensitive man spends a moment with a wise man, he soon knows the path of wisdom, as the tongue knows the taste of soup.

Dhammapada, 64-65

(16) The Introduction of Buddhism into the Theravada Countries

i. Ceylon (Sri Lanka)

Buddhism was brought to what was then called Ceylon in the third century B.C. by Mahinda and Sanghamitta, the son and daughter of the Indian Buddhist King Ashoka. The king of Ceylon, Devānampiya Tissa became a Buddhist and built the Mahāvihāra ("great monastery") in his capital Anurādhapura, where a branch of the Bodhi-tree, brought by Sanghamitta from Bodh-Gayā to Ceylon, was planted, and is still alive today. For many centuries this monastery remained the center of *Theravāda* Buddhism. *Mahāyāna* and Tantric schools, which had monasteries at Abhayagiri and Jetavana, also flourished for several centuries, but *Theravāda* prevailed, thanks in large part to the influence of the great Indian Buddhist sage Buddhaghosha who had migrated to Ceylon at the beginning of the fifth century. There was a great upsurge of *Theravāda* Buddhism at Polonnaruwa in the eleventh century, and since the time of King Parakkambahu in the twelfth century, Buddhism in Sri Lanka has been more or less exclusively *Theravāda*.

ii. Burma

One tradition says that Buddhism was taken from India to Burma in the time of the Buddha by two merchants who brought with them some of the Buddha's hair, which is conserved to this day in the Shwedagon Pagoda in Rangoon. Another tradition says that Buddhism spread to Burma in the third century B.C. during the reign of the Indian King Ashoka. For several centuries *Theravāda* and *Mahāyāna* schools co-existed, but from the eleventh century onwards the entire country has been *Theravāda*.

iii. Siam (Thailand)

Between the first and thirteenth centuries there were widespread Indian commercial links with, and colonization of, south-east Asia, in the areas which comprise Siam, Cambodia, Laos, and Vietnam, as well as Malaysia, Sumatra, Java, Borneo, and Bali. Hinduism flourished in all of these countries. As far as Thailand is concerned, it is believed that Buddhism of the *Theravāda* type spread there from Burma between the third and sixth centuries. The *Mahāyāna* school also flourished amongst the Thais during the immediately succeeding centuries. In the thirteenth century, the Thai kingdom of Sukhodaya was founded, which became known as the "cradle of Thailandese civilization". Buddhism of the *Theravāda* school prevailed over Hinduism and *Mahāyāna* Buddhism, and has since then predominated in Siam.

iv. Cambodia

Both *Hīnayāna* and *Mahāyāna* Buddhism are known to have been present in Cambodia from the third century onwards, having first entered the country from Siam and later from Ceylon. *Mahāyāna* Buddhism sometimes merged, and sometimes contended, with Shaivite Hinduism. With the renaissance of Buddhism in Ceylon in the Polonnaruwa period (eleventh century), successive waves of Buddhist influence overran the south-east Asian countries and, by the thirteenth century, under the patronage of the Cambodian royal house, *Theravāda* Buddhism made decisive gains over the other two traditions. Since that time *Theravāda* Buddhism has been the dominant religion in Cambodia.

v. Laos

The history of Buddhism in Laos closely parallels that of Cambodia. Hinduism and the two main schools of Buddhism co-existed in the earlier centuries. In the eleventh century, influences from Ceylon contributed to the success of *Theravāda* Buddhism, and from the thirteenth century onwards it has been the predominant religion in Laos.

The world is afflicted with death and decay, therefore the wise do not grieve, knowing the terms of the world.
                              Buddhaghosha (fifth century, A.D.)

Shwedagon Pagoda, Burma, 6th century B.C.

The Wat Phra Singh Temple, Thailand, 14th century

Angkor Wat, Cambodia, 12th century

Wat Xieng Thong, Laos, 16th century

Map of India and Neighboring Countries
(circa 1900)

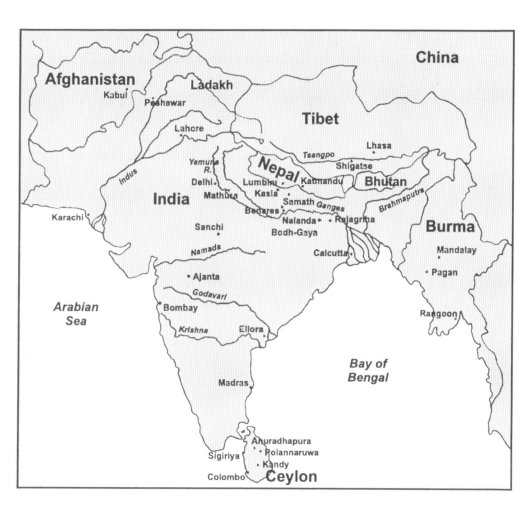

Potala Palace, Lhasa,Tibet

Husbands should respect their wives, and comply as far as possible with their requests. They should not commit adultery. They should give their wives full charge of the home, and supply them with fine clothes and jewelry as far as their means permit. Wives should be thorough in their duties, gentle and kind to the whole household, chaste, and careful in housekeeping, and should carry out their work with skill and enthusiasm.

A man should be generous to his friends, speak kindly to them, act in their interests in every way possible, treat them as his equals, and keep his word to them. They in turn should watch over his interests and property, take care of him when he is off his guard, stand by him and help him in time of trouble, and respect other members of his family.

Employers should treat their servants and workpeople decently. They should not be given tasks beyond their strength. They should receive adequate food and wages, be cared for in time of sickness and infirmity, and be given regular holidays and bonuses in time of prosperity. They should rise early and go to bed late in the service of their master, be content with their just wages, work thoroughly, and maintain their master's reputation.

Dīgha-Nikāya, iii, 181ff

(17) Tibet

i. The Introduction of Buddhism into Tibet

Buddhism was first introduced into Tibet in the seventh century A.D. by King Songtsen Gampo, who was looked on as an incarnation of Avalokiteshvara (Chenrezig). Two princesses whom he married, one from Nepal and one from China, were considered to be incarnations of the supreme feminine principle Tārā—respectively "green Tārā" and "white Tārā", representing two complementary modes of celestial favors. (See p. 72.)

For a time Buddhism contended with the earlier religion of Bön, but in 791 A.D. King Trisong Detsen issued an edict declaring Buddhism to be the official religion of the country. The king was still faced with the rivalry of two Buddhist sects, the "Gradual Path" (combining elements of *Sarvāstivāda* and *Vajrayāna*) which had come from India and the "Sudden Path" (*Dhyāna* or *Ch'an*) which had come from China. The king invited the Indian monk Kamalashīla and the Chinese monk Mahāyāna to expound before him their respective viewpoints. In 794, after two years of vigorous debate, the king decided in favor of the Indian monk and his doctrines, and the Chinese monk was unceremoniously expelled. *Ch'an* Buddhism disappeared from Tibet, and *Sarvāstivāda* and especially *Vajrayāna* henceforth predominated.

In the succeeding centuries, several characteristically Tibetan schools of Buddhism developed. The fortunes of Buddhism oscillated, but Buddhism in Tibet was given new life in the eleventh century by the Indian sage Atīsha.

*
* *

One should not be rash or hasty in one's desire to teach others as long as one has not realized the truth oneself; otherwise one runs the risk of being a blind man leading the blind.

Milarepa

ii. The Four Main Schools

The four main schools or spiritual orders of Tibetan Buddhism (along with their founders and some of the principal figures associated with them) are as follows:

1. The Nyingma School (eighth century)

The Indian sage Padmasambhava, who had taught at the Buddhist university of Nālandā in India, migrated to Tibet, where he founded the *Nyingma* order, which incorporated elements from *Sarvāstivāda* and *Vajrayāna*. *Sarvāstivāda* (see p. 53) may be regarded as a transitional stage between *Hīnayāna* and *Mahāyāna*. The followers of this order, *Nyingma-pas* ("Old-style Ones"), are known as "Red Hats". They are adherents of the school of "Great Perfection" (*Dzogchen*) or "Supreme Yoga" (*Atiyoga*). The *Nyingma* order—to a greater extent than any of the other orders mentioned below—also assimilated certain elements from the older Bön religion.

2. The Sakya School (eleventh century)

Koncho Gyepo Khön was the founder of the *Sakya* ("Gray Earth") order, which is devoted to the transmission of a cycle of *Vajrayāna* teachings known as *Lamdre* ("Path and Goal"). Amongst its leading gurus (whom *Sakya-pas* regard as incarnations of Avalokiteshvara) were Sachen Kunga Nyingpo (twelfth century) and Sakya Pandita (thirteenth century).

3. The Kagyü School (eleventh century)

Marpa and Milarepa were the founders of the *Kagyü* order. Its followers, *Kagyü-pas* ("Transmitters of the Word"), are adherents of the school of the "Great Symbol" (*Mahāmudrā*). Marpa and Milarepa followed the "Diamond Vehicle" (*Vajrayāna*—also known as *Mantrayāna* or *Tantrayāna*), which they had learned from the Indian masters Tilopa and Nāropa at Nālandā. An off-shoot of the *Kagyü* school is the *Karma-Kagyü* school, whose members, *Karma-Kagyü -pas*, are known as "Black Hats". Their spiritual head is the *Karmapa*.

4. The Gelug School (fourteenth century)

Tsongkhapa was the founder of the *Gelug* order. The *Gelug-pas* ("Followers of the Virtuous Path") are known as "Yellow Hats". This order developed from the much earlier *Kadam* order ("Linked by the Doctrine"), which had been founded in the eleventh century by the Indian Atīsha. *Gelug-pas* are adherents of the school of the "Middle Way" (*Mādhyamika*), which originated in India under Nāgārjuna in the second century. This is now the "established" order in Tibet, of which the Dalai Lama is the spiritual head.[1]

Vajra mandala, Tibet, 16th century

As rain does not break through a well-thatched house, passion will not break through a well-reflecting mind.
Khuddaka-Nikāya, Dhammapada, 14

[1] See Marco Pallis, *Peaks and Lamas* (London: Frank Cass, 1974).

The principal luminaries in the Tibetan Buddhist firmament may be listed chronologically as follows:

Nāgārjuna [Indian] (second century)

King Songtsen Gampo (seventh century)

King Trisong Detsen (eighth century)

Shāntirakshita [Indian] (eighth century)

Padmasambhava [Indian] (eighth century)—*Nyingma* order—"Red Hats"

Rinchen Zangpo (tenth century) ["the Great Translator"]

Atīsha Dipamkara Shrī Jñāna [Indian] (eleventh century)

Koncho Gyepo Khön (eleventh century)—*Sakya* order—"Gray Earth"

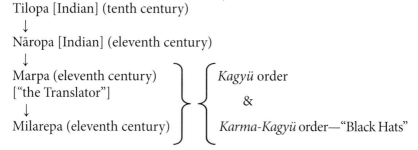

Tilopa [Indian] (tenth century)
↓
Nāropa [Indian] (eleventh century)
↓
Marpa (eleventh century)   *Kagyü* order
["the Translator"]   &
↓
Milarepa (eleventh century)   *Karma-Kagyü* order—"Black Hats"

Tsongkhapa (fourteenth-fifteenth century)—*Gelug* order—"Yellow Hats"

He who knoweth the precepts by heart, but faileth to practice them, is like unto one who lighteth a lamp and then shutteth his eyes.

The Ocean of Light for the Wise

iii. Tantra

In Buddhism, there are not only the *Hīnayāna* and *Mahāyāna* schools. There is also a branch of *Mahāyāna*, namely *Vajrayāna* or *Tantrayāna*, which, because of its importance, is called the "Third School" or the "Third Setting in Motion of the Wheel of the Law". *Vajrayāna* spread from India to Tibet in the eleventh century, and became of particular importance in the latter country.

Buddhism in general looks on the world as an exile; it sees it under its negative aspect of corruptibility and temptation—and so of suffering. *Tantra*, on the contrary, sees the world positively as theophany or symbol; it sees through the forms to the essences. Its spiritual way is union with the celestial archetypes of created things. In the words of Frithjof Schuon: "*Tantra* is the spiritualization—or interiorization—of beauty, and also of natural pleasures, by virtue of the metaphysical transparency of phenomena. In a word: *Tantra* is nobility of sentiments and experiences; it excludes all excess and goes hand in hand with sobriety; it is a sense of archetypes, a return to essences and primordiality."[2]

The metaphysical doctrine and spiritual practice of *tantra* is based on the masculine and feminine principles or "poles", known in Vedānta as *purusha* and *prakriti*. In Hinduism, these are represented or symbolized by Shiva and his Consort (*Shakti*) Kali. In *Mahāyāna* Buddhism in general, and in Tibetan Buddhism in particular, the masculine and feminine principles appear in the form of the following pairs:

Masculine	Feminine
Upāya ("Formal doctrine and method")	*Prajñā* ("Formless wisdom")
Vajra ("Lightning", "Diamond")	*Garbha* ("Womb")
Dorje ("Thunderbolt scepter")	*Drilbu* ("Handbell")
Mani ("Jewel")	*Padma* ("Lotus")
YAB ("Father")	YUM ("Mother")
intellectuality	spirituality

---

[2] Unpublished text, no. 1042.

This polarity (and its resolution) evokes the doctrine implicit in one of the Hindu names for God, namely *Sat-Chit-Ānanda*, often translated as "Being-Consciousness-Bliss". *In divinis* this Ternary means "Object-Subject-Union" and, spiritually or operatively, it can be rendered as "Beloved-Lover-Love" and other analogous ternaries:

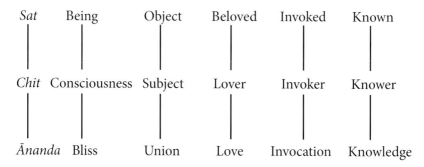

Sat	Being	Object	Beloved	Invoked	Known
Chit	Consciousness	Subject	Lover	Invoker	Knower
Ānanda	Bliss	Union	Love	Invocation	Knowledge

In this context, the first row is seen as the "feminine" element (*prajñā*), the second row as the "masculine" element (*upāya*), and the third row as the union between them (*sukha*).

Metaphysically, it can be said that *saṃsāra* (the world) "is" *Nirvāna* (the Divine State). This is because Reality is one, and the Principle of *saṃsāra* is *Nirvāna*. Also, and for the same reason, the distinction can be bridged in unitive prayer: "The Kingdom of Heaven is within you." For fallen man, however, the situation is quite different: *saṃsāra* is very far from *Nirvāna*. Hence the Buddha's central message: "I teach two things, O disciples, suffering and release from suffering." In theistic terms, one can say that existence, by definition, involves separation from the Divine Source. God created the world so that "other-than-God" could know Him. The purpose of existence is precisely the work of return; were it not so, existence would have no meaning. This work is compounded of faith and prayer, and rendered possible by the saving grace of the *Avatāra*. In *Vajrayāna* Buddhism, *tantra* is the Way of Return.

The operative side of tantric doctrine resides essentially in the invocatory spiritual method (*mantrayāna*) referred to on pp. 79-80, namely *Buddhānusmriti* ("remembrance of the Buddha"). In Christianity, the analogous method finds its scriptural basis in the text "Whoever shall call upon the Name of the Lord shall be saved" (Romans, 10:13). This practice takes the form of the constant or frequent invocation of a sacred formula or *mantra*, the sacramental power of which derives from the Name (or Names) of the Divinity which it contains. If meditation is

T'hanka of Guhyasamāja, a form of Akshobya Buddha,
in union with his consort Sparshavajrā, Central Tibet, 17th century

Green Tārā, Mongolia, early 18th century

the emptying of the mind of worldly things, invocation is the filling of the mind (and heart) with a revealed Divine Name and its saving grace.

The masculine and feminine principles of *tantra* are present in the Names contained in the *Mani-Mantra*, the central invocatory prayer of Tibetan Buddhism, namely, *Om Mani Padme Hum*: "O Thou Jewel in the Lotus, hail." The Jewel may be interpreted as Avalokiteshvara (the Bodhisattva representing the Buddha's Mercy or Compassion) and the Lotus as his feminine counterpart Tārā. The Lotus (*padma*) is the existential or "horizontal" support for the "vertical" or "axial" Jewel (*mani*).

The Lotus is thus the symbol of the pure and humble human soul (viewed as feminine and "horizontal") that opens out its petals (i.e. acquires the fundamental spiritual virtues) so that it may attract, and become the fitting vehicle of, the Jewel of Buddheic grace (viewed as masculine and "vertical"). This symbolism is identical to that of weaving, in which the weft (horizontal) and the warp (vertical) are in the same "sexual" relationship to one another. "Weaving" is in fact the literal meaning of the word *tantra*.

There is an obvious analogy between the Tibetan formula and similar invocatory prayers in other religions, such as *Sītā-Rām* in Hinduism and *Jesu-Maria* in Catholicism.

As indicated in the table on the preceding page, the union of the "Subject" with the "Object", of the Invoker with the Invoked, of the Lover (masculine) with the Beloved (feminine) results in *Ānanda* or "Bliss". In Buddhist *tantra* this spiritual union is called *Mahāsukha* ("the Great Bliss"). This is symbolized in Tibetan art by the tantric statue of *Yab-Yum* (literally "father-mother"), which portrays the loving union of the masculine and the feminine principles.

The *mantra* Om Mani Padme Hum
("O Thou Jewel in the Lotus, hail!")

His Holiness the 13th Dalai Lama, *lama tulku* of Avalokiteshvara

Take heed of the lives of the saints, the law of karma, the miseries of worldly existence . . . , the certainty of death, and the uncertainty of the time of death. Weigh these things in your minds, and devote yourselves to the study and practice of Remembrance.

Milarepa[3]

---

[3] In the above quotation, Remembrance means "remembrance of the Buddha" (*Buddhānusmriti*) through the way of invocatory prayer (*mantrayāna*).

iv. The Panchen Lama and the Dalai Lama

In order to understand the roles of the Panchen Lama and the Dalai Lama, it is necessary to take into account the "celestial principles" (i.e., the Buddha or Bodhisattva) which they represent. These are respectively Amitābha Buddha and Avalokiteshvara. (See the tables on pp. 72-73.)

Amitābha Buddha is the Buddha (or Aspect of the one and universal Buddha) who presides over the "Western Paradise" (i.e. the state entered by those who achieve salvation through the invocation of the Name of Amitābha).

Avalokiteshvara (known as "Chenrezig" in Tibetan) is the Bodhisattva who represents one of the main qualities of Amitābha, namely Mercy or Compassion. Avalokiteshvara is said to emerge from the forehead of Amitābha.

A *lama tulku* is a human being who has the function of incarnating a "celestial principle". (The various *lama tulku*s are sometimes, perhaps misleadingly, referred to as "Living Buddhas".) The Panchen Lama, whose traditional residence is in Shigatse, is the *lama tulku* who incarnates Amitābha (the Buddha of the "Western Paradise"). The Dalai Lama, whose traditional residence is in Lhasa, is the *lama tulku* who incarnates Avalokiteshvara (the Bodhisattva of Mercy or Compassion).

Since Avalokiteshvara is hierarchically inferior to Amitābha, the Dalai Lama is hierarchically inferior to the Panchen Lama. But this does not detract from the importance in practice of the Dalai Lama, who has the specific function of "Protector of Tibet". He fulfills this function, not merely by being both temporal ruler and supreme religious authority, but also by exercising what is known in the Buddhist world as an "activity of presence". As *lama tulku* of Avalokiteshvara or Chenrezig (the Bodhisattva of Compassion), the Dalai Lama is the incarnation of this "celestial principle", and through him, it radiates, protectively, over the Tibetan people and their religion. It is this "activity of presence" that is the essential role of the Dalai Lama.

The office of *lama tulku* of Chenrezig is transmitted from one Dalai Lama to the next by means of a certain traditional process which is described by Heinrich Harrer in his book *Seven Years in Tibet*.

If the Dalai Lama possesses the providential function of Protector of Tibet, it may be asked why it was possible for him to be displaced from office, expelled from Tibet, and for his country and religion to have been ravaged by the Chinese communists. The answer to this is that everything under the sun, including even a great spiritual dynasty, has both a beginning and an end, and, when the appointed time has come, must needs pass away. However the celestial principle which the Dalai Lamas incarnated is imperishable. One recalls the saying of Christ: "Heaven and earth will pass away, but My words will not pass away."

Young Tibetan Buddhist woman

In other living creatures, ignorance of Self is nature; in man it is a vice.

The Buddha

(18) China

i. The Introduction of Buddhism into China

Buddhism was introduced into China during the first century A.D. and the immediately succeeding centuries. It is said traditionally that this was on the order of the mythical Yellow Emperor, Fu-Hsi, and the venerable Founder of Taoism, Lao Tzu, who were regarded as possessing immortality.

On the one hand, Indian Buddhist monks entered China as missionaries. On the other hand, Chinese pilgrims traveled to India to visit the earliest and most sacred Buddhist shrines and to learn about Buddhism, thereafter returning to their own country to spread the message. From that time onwards, in China, Buddhism and the indigenous traditions of Confucianism and Taoism were called "the Three Teachings" or "the Three Religions".

Early in the fifth century A.D., Fa-Hsien, after an arduous journey through central Asia, reached India. He spent fifteen years in India and Ceylon and compiled a detailed account of Buddhism that is renowned in China to this day. In the year 520 A.D., Bodhidharma left India and became the first patriarch of *Ch'an* Buddhism in China. In the seventh century, during the T'ang Dynasty, the monk Hsüan-Tsang traveled through East Turkestan and Afghanistan to India, eventually returning to China laden with Buddhist books and manuscripts, hundreds of which he translated into Chinese.

The *Vajrayāna* or tantric doctrines were brought to China (under the name of *Mi-tsung*) by the three Indian masters Shubhākarasimha (637-735), Vajrabodhi (663-723), and Amoghavajra (705-774).

During the sixth to ninth centuries (the Sui and T'ang dynasties), several great schools of Chinese Buddhism developed. These are:

School	Literal Meaning	Founder	School in Japan
Hua-yen	"Flower Garland"	Fa-tsang (643-712)	Kegon
Tien-Tai	"Heavenly Terrace"	Chih-i (538-597)	Tendai
Mi-tsung	"School of Secrets"	Shubhākarasimha (637-735)	Shingon
Ch'an	"Contemplation"	Bodhidharma (470-543)	Zen
Ching-t'u	"Pure Land"	Tan-Luan (476-542)	Jōdo
Fa-hsiang	"Dharma-Character"	Hsüan-Tsang (600-664)	Hossō

The "Dharma-Character" school (*Fa-hsiang* in Chinese; *Hossō* in Japanese) was also known as the "Consciousness-Only" school (*Wei-shih* in Chinese; *Yuishiki* in Japanese). It never flourished in Japan to the extent that it did in China.

For the Indian precursors of some of the Chinese schools, and for fuller information on the Japanese schools or sects, see pp. 55, 58, 116-117, and 121.

Shen Zhou, *Poet on a Mountain Top*, Ming Dynasty, China

Whoever speaks or acts with an impure mind, him sorrow follows, as the wheel follows the steps of the ox that draws the cart.
Dhammapada, 2

Statue of Bodhisattva Kwan-Yin, Shanxi, China, 1100

It is useless to try to force to believe those who will not, for even the Buddha cannot do that.

Hōnen

ii. The Chinese Dynasties

c. 3700 B.C.-2000 B.C.	Neolithic culture	*c. 2800 B.C. Fu-Hsi, the First Emperor, author of the* I Ching
c. 1766 B.C.-1122 B.C.	Shang-Yin Dynasty	
1122 B.C.-221 B.C.	Chou Dynasty	*c. 563 B.C. birth of the Buddha in North India*

c. 722 B.C.-481 B.C.   Spring and Autumn Annals

c. 481 B.C.-221 B.C.   Warring States

221 B.C.-206 B.C.   Ch'in Dynasty (Empire of Shih Huang Ti)

206 B.C.-220 A.D.	Han Dynasty	*introduction of Buddhism in the first and succeeding centuries A.D.*
220 A.D.-589 A.D.	Six Dynasties	
220 A.D.-280 A.D.	Three Kingdoms	

386 A.D.-589 A.D.   North [Wei Tartars] (386 A.D.-581 A.D.)

386 A.D.-535 A.D.	North: Wei Tartars	*in the fourth century Fa-Hsien wrote an account of Indian Buddhism*

535 A.D.-557 A.D.   Western Wei

557 A.D.-581 A.D.   Northern Chou

534 A.D.-550 A.D.   Eastern Wei

550 A.D.-577 A.D.   Northern Ch'i

South [Native Dynasties] (420 A.D.-589 A.D.)

420 A.D.-478 A.D.   Liu Sung

479 A.D.-501 A.D.   Southern Ch'i

502 A.D.-556 A.D.	Liang	*in 520 A.D. Bodhidharma became the first patriarch of Ch'an*
557 A.D.-589 A.D.	Ch'en	
581 A.D.-618 A.D.	Sui Dynasty	*in the seventh century Hsüan-Tsang translated voluminous Buddhist literature from India*
618 A.D.-906 A.D.	T'ang Dynasty	
907 A.D.-960 A.D.	Five Dynastics	
960 A.D-1279 A.D.	Sung Dynasty	
1280 A.D.-1368 A.D.	Yüan Dynasty [Mongol]	
1368 A.D.-1644 A.D.	Ming Dynasty	

1368 A.D.-1398 A.D.	Hung Wu
1403 A.D.-1424 A.D.	Yung Lo
1426 A.D.-1435 A.D.	Hsüan Tē
1465 A.D.-1487 A.D.	Ch'ĕng Hua
1488 A.D.-1505 A.D.	Hung Chih
1506 A.D.-1521 A.D.	Chēng Tē
1522 A.D.-1566 A.D.	Chia Ching
1567 A.D.-1572 A.D.	Lung Ch'ing
1573 A.D-1620 A.D.	Wan Li

1644 A.D.-1912 A.D.	Ch'ing Dynasty [Manchu]

1662 A.D.-1722 A.D.	K'ang Hsi
1723 A.D.-1735 A.D.	Yung Chēng
1736 A.D.-1795 A.D.	Ch'ien Lung

The invocatory formula of the Pure Land school in Sanskrit
(See pp. 79-80.)
Namo 'mitābhaya Buddhāya
"I take refuge in the Buddha of Infinite Light"

नमो अमिताभाय बुद्धाय

Whoever recites the Name of Amitābha Buddha, whether in the present or in the future, will surely see the Buddha Amitābha and never become separated from him. By reason of that association, just as one associating with a maker of perfumes becomes permeated with the same perfumes, so he will become perfumed by Amitābha's compassion, and will become enlightened without resort to any other expedient means.

Surangama Sūtra

iii. Chinese Calligraphy

The invocatory formula of the Pure Land school in Chinese
Na-mu O-mi-t'o Fu' (Chinese)
Namu Amida Butsu (Japanese)
"I take refuge in the Buddha of Infinite Light"

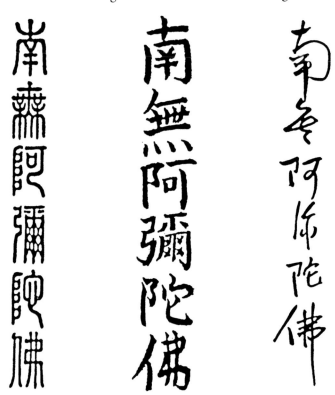

Archaic or seal script   Regular or standard script   Cursive script

Chinese: chüan-shu   *Chinese*: k'ai-shu or chēn-shu   *Chinese*: ts'ao-shu
Japanese: tensho   *Japanese*: kaisho or shinsho   *Japanese*: sosho

This script is close to the writing that has its origin with the first Chinese Emperor Fu-Hsi in the third millennium B.C.

Map of China and Neighboring Countries
(circa 1900)

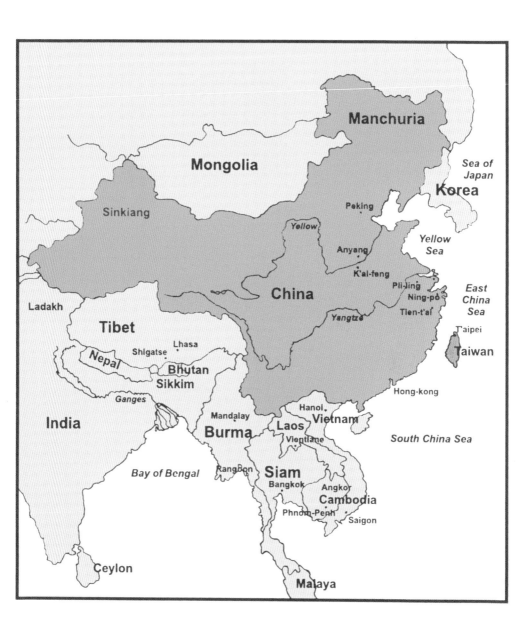

(19) Korea

i. The Introduction of Buddhism into Korea

Buddhism was introduced into Korea from China in the fourth century A.D. during the period of the Three Kingdoms. It gradually grew and flourished, and within a few centuries had reached a high peak. During the Great Silla Period, thanks to Buddhism, the whole peninsula experienced a virtual "golden age", which is especially notable in art. During the Yi (Chosōn) Dynasty, the Confucian social system was introduced.

In 552 A.D., Buddhism was transmitted from the Korean kingdom of Paekche to Japan. Much of the early Buddhist art in Japan is considered to be the work of Korean craftsmen and their Japanese pupils.

Maitreya Buddha, Great Silla period, Korea, 7th century

Wishing to entice the blind,
The Buddha playfully let words escape from his golden mouth;
Heaven and earth are filled, ever since, with entangling briars!
Dai-o Kokushi

ii. The Korean Dynasties

2333 B.C.	legendary foundation, by the half-human, half-divine Tan-gun, of the nation from which Koreans are descended
108 B.C.-313 A.D.	Chinese colonies in Korea
57 B.C.-668 A.D.	Three Kingdoms

37 B.C.-668 A.D. Koguryō Dynasty

18 B.C.-663 A.D. Paekche Dynasty

57 B.C.-68 A.D. Old Silla Dynasty

668 A.D.-935 A.D.	Great Silla Dynasty
918 A.D.-1392 A.D.	Koryō Dynasty
1392 A.D.-1910 A.D.	Yi Dynasty (Chosōn Kingdom)
1910 A.D.-1945 A.D.	Korea annexed by Japan
1945 A.D.	end of Japanese rule

Map of Korea and Japan
(circa 1900)

Buddha statue of gilded wood, Japan
Ethnological Museum, Basle, Switzerland

(20) Japan

i. The Introduction of Buddhism into Japan

Buddhism was first introduced into Japan from the Korean kingdom of Paekche (Kudara) during the Asuka Period (sixth century A.D.) by Shōtoko Taishi, regent of his aunt, the Empress Suiko. The exact date is traditionally said to have been 552 A.D. The magnificent early Buddhist works of art in the seventh century monastery of Hōryū-ji, near Nara in Japan, are considered to have been produced by Korean sculptors and craftsmen as well as by their Japanese pupils.

It is remarkable how rapidly the transmission of Buddhist teachings over immense distances could take place. For example, the Indian master of the *Vajrayāna* school, Vajrabodhi, arrived in China in 720 A.D. His chosen disciple was Amoghavajra (Pu-k'ung), and the latter's primary successor was the Japanese Kōbō Daishi (Kūkai), who returned to Japan at the beginning of the ninth century, where he founded the Shingon sect. All this (from India, via China, to Japan) happened within the space of about 80 years.

The Japanese historical periods are shown on the next page.

The priest Kōbō Daishi as a child, Japan, 14th century

Make the practice of Nembutsu [*the invocation of the saving Name of the Buddha*] *the chief thing in life. Lay aside everything that may interfere with it.*

Hōnen

ii. The Japanese Periods

600 B.C.	Foundation of the Japanese Empire by Jimmu Tennō
600 B.C.-c. 250 B.C.	Jōmon Period
c. 250 B.C.-c. 250 A.D.	Yayoi Period
c. 250 A.D.-c. 552 A.D.	Kofun Period
552 A.D.-645 A.D.	Asuka Period

introduction of Buddhism

645 A.D.-794 A.D.	Nara Period	
	645 A.D.-710 A.D.	Hakuhō Period
	711 A.D.-794 A.D.	Tempyō Period
794 A.D.-1185 A.D.	Heian Period	
	794 A.D.-897 A.D.	Jōgan Period
	898 A.D.-1185 A.D.	Fujiwara Period
1185 A.D.-1333 A.D.	Kamakura Period	
1333 A.D.-1392 A.D.	Nambokuchō Period	
1392 A.D.-1568 A.D.	Muromachi Period	
1568 A.D.-1615 A.D.	Momoyama Period	
1615 A.D.-1868 A.D.	Edo Period	
	1615 A.D.-1688 A.D.	Early Edo Period
	1688 A.D.-1764 A.D.	Middle Edo Period
	1764 A.D.-1868 A.D.	Later Edo Period
1868 A.D.-present	Modern Japan	
	1868 A.D.-1912 A.D.	Meiji era
	1912 A.D.-1926 A.D.	Taishō era
	1926 A.D.-present	Shōwa era

iii. A Selection of Haiku (Japanese 17-syllable Poems)[1]

My ears had found the sermon dull and stale;
But in the woods outside—the nightingale!
                            Masaoka Shiki (1866-1902)

Without a word of warning, look, alone
Above the autumn clouds, Mount Fuji's cone!
                            Kamijima Onitsura (1660-1738)

O timid snail, by nature weak and lowly,
Crawl up the cone of Fuji slowly, slowly. . . .
                            Kobayashi Issa (1763-1827)

Between the washing-bowls at birth and death,
All that I uttered: what a waste of breath!
                            Kobayashi Issa (1763-1827)

I have seen moon and blossoms, now I go
To view the last and lovliest: the snow.
                            Rippo (1600-1669)[2]

---

[1] From *A Net of Fireflies*, translations by Harold Stewart (Rutland, Vermont, and Tokyo, Japan: Charles E. Tuttle Company, 1960).

[2] Written by the poet on his death-bed. Moon and blossoms are forms. The snow is pure Substance.

iv. The Sects of Japanese Buddhism

The Japanese masters Dengyō-Daishi (Saichō) (767-822) and Kōbō Daishi (Kūkai) (774-835) were acquainted with each other, but of differing perspectives. Both studied in China and both returned to Japan at the beginning of the ninth century A.D. Dengyō Daishi founded the Tendai sect, the name of which comes from the Chinese Mount *Tien-t'ai* ("Heavenly Terrace") and Kōbō Daishi founded the Shingon sect, the name coming from the Chinese *Chen-yen* ("True Word").

The Tendai school includes a wide variety of spiritual practices, whereas other schools tend to focus on one or another of them. Thus Tendai incorporates liturgical rites (which are characteristic of the Shingon school), "sitting meditation" or *zazen* (on which the Zen school lays emphasis), and *mantra*s such as the *nembutsu* (of the *Jōdo* or "Pure Land" school).

Tendai is known as the school of teaching and study (of the *sūtra*s). The Patron of the school is the Bodhisattva known in Japanese as *Fudō-Myō-ō* (Sanskrit: *Achala Vidyārāja*, "the Unshakable King of Knowledge"), viewed as a manifestation of *Dainichi Nyorai* (Sanskrit: *Dharmakāya* or *Mahāvairochana*)—the Supreme Reality. Fudō is the awesome opponent of the world's inequities, stupor, and indifference to truth. The fire of his righteous anger burns up error and sin while illuminating the darkest corners of *samsāra*.

In Zen (see pp. 54-55, 61, and 63), a well-known feature is the *kōan*, the purpose of which is to stimulate *satori* (sudden illumination, unitive knowledge or gnosis, spiritual realization). The *kōan* is usually a phrase from Scripture, often paradoxical in nature, and its comprehension involves the transcending of discursive thought.

The central spiritual practice of *Jōdo*, namely *nembutsu*, has been described on pp. 79-80.

In the following table of some of the major Japanese Buddhist sects or schools, the names of the founders are given within brackets. It should be said once again that these various "sects" represent varying angles of vision with regard to the original Buddhist revelation and all of them, though they sometimes differ greatly one from another, are intrinsically orthodox.

Some of the Major Sects of Japanese Buddhism[1]

The founders' names are given within parentheses. For the antecedent and corresponding Chinese sects, see p. 101.

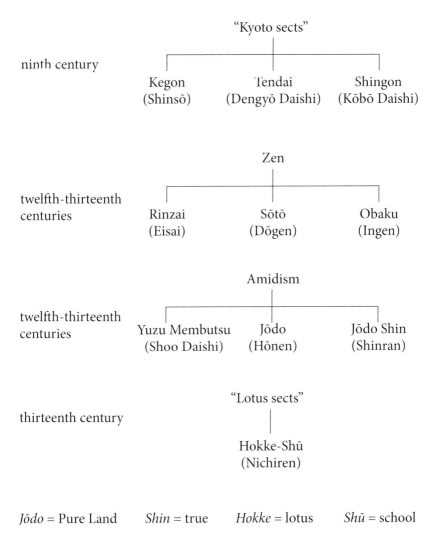

"Kyoto sects"

ninth century

| Kegon (Shinsō) | Tendai (Dengyō Daishi) | Shingon (Kōbō Daishi) |

Zen

twelfth-thirteenth centuries

| Rinzai (Eisai) | Sōtō (Dōgen) | Obaku (Ingen) |

Amidism

twelfth-thirteenth centuries

| Yuzu Membutsu (Shoo Daishi) | Jōdo (Hōnen) | Jōdo Shin (Shinran) |

"Lotus sects"

thirteenth century

Hokke-Shū (Nichiren)

Jōdo = Pure Land   *Shin* = true   *Hokke* = lotus   *Shū* = school

[1] See E. Steinilber and Kuni Matsuo, *Les Sectes Bouddhiques Japonaises* (Paris: Crès, 1930).

Zen rock garden, Nanzenji Temple, Japan

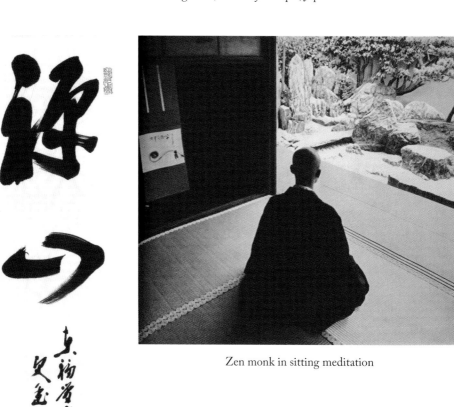

Zen monk in sitting meditation

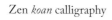

Zen *koan* calligraphy

Amida Buddha rising from behind the mountains like a Sun of Compassion, Konkaikomyo-ji, Kyoto, Japan, 13th century

Amida Buddha, hanging scroll, gold on silk, Japan, 19th century

Bodhisattva Kwannon,
lacquered and gilt wood, Japan, 14th century

*Even though, through the days and years of your life, you have
piled up much merit by the practice of the Nembutsu, if at the
time of death you come under the spell of some evil, give way to
an evil heart, lose faith in and cease practicing the Nembutsu,
you will lose birth into the Pure Land immediately after death
. . . . This is a most terrible thing to contemplate and one which
no words can describe.*

Hōnen

v. Summary of Some Buddhist Schools or Sects[1]

Indian, Chinese, and Japanese

Sanskrit	Chinese	Literal Meaning	Japanese
Avatamsaka	Hua-yen	"Flower Garland"	Kegon
—	Tien-T'ai	"Heavenly Terrace"	Tendai
Vajrayāna	Mi-tsung	"School of Secrets"	Shingon
Dhyāna	Ch'an	"Contemplation"	Zen
Sukhāvatī	Ching-t'u	"Pure Land"	Jōdo
Yogāchāra	Fa-hsiang	"Dharma-Character"	Hossō
Chitta-matra	Wei-shih	"Consciousness-Only"	Yuishiki

Tibetan

(1) Nyingma	"Red Hats"
(2) Sakya	"Gray Hats"
(3) Kagyü &	
Karma-Kagyü	"Black Hats"
(4) Gelug	"Yellow Hats"

The five *Dhyāni-Buddha*s, Japan, 17th-18th century
Ethnological Museum, Leiden, Netherlands

[1] For fuller details see pp. 54-55, 90-91, 101, and 116-117.

T'hanka of Mt. Meru and the Buddhist universe, Bhutan, 19th century

A group of people were conversing about the future life. Some said that fish-eaters would be born into the Pure Land, others said that they would not. Hōnen overheard them and said: "If it is a case of eating fish, cormorants would be born into the Pure Land, and if it is a case of not eating fish, monkeys would be so born. But I am sure that whether a man eats fish or not, if he only calls upon the Sacred Name, he will be born into the Pure Land."

Hōnen

(21) The Question of Reincarnation

In Buddhism, as in Hinduism, there are elaborate theories regarding cosmic cycles, "worlds", "heavens", and "hells". Linked with these is the doctrine of transmigration—or multiple births and rebirths—frequently referred to as "reincarnation".

In the modern West, the notion of "reincarnation" has been adopted by many cultists, who, in the grossest manner imaginable, profess to believe in it literally, envisaging a series of human rebirths in this world. It is true that a literal attitude towards transmigration is also to be found among the Hindu and Buddhist masses, and indeed such a belief derives from a literal interpretation of the respective scriptures. However, the most simple Asian peasant, even if he looks on transmigration literally, has an infinitely more subtle intuition of the moral and spiritual implications of this doctrine than the grotesque cultists of the West. In Asia, a literalist attitude towards transmigration is not only harmless, but may even be beneficial. The gross "reincarnation-ism" of renegade Christian pseudo-esoterists, on the other hand, is immensely harmful for themselves and others.

For a Buddhist, a literal belief in transmigration is like a Christian believing that hell is a fiery furnace down below. It may not be strictly true—and yet it is not false either, because the image is one which is adequate to the deeper (and more complex) truth in question and, being so, has had a salutary moral and spiritual effect for countless generations.

The point is that elements plucked from one religious imagery (though in themselves "figures of truth") are frequently not transplantable to another; above all, they cannot be transplanted, without grave results, from a traditional world into the chaotic modern world, where there is minimal religious instruction, minimal religious sensibility, and a minimal will to understand.

The Hindu and Buddhist doctrine of transmigration refers to the posthumous journeying of the unsanctified soul through an indefinite series of "peripheral" or "central" (but, quite emphatically, non-terrestrial) states: René Guénon often emphasized that "no being of any kind can pass through the same state twice". The term "peripheral" is used to indicate states which are analogous to animals or even plants in this world, and the term "central" is used to indicate states which are analogous to the human state.

In some respects, transmigration may be regarded as the mytho-
logical analogue of the theological doctrine of purgatory—with the
important difference, however, that, according to the Catholic doctrine, a soul in purgatory has definitively retained its "central" state
and is assured of eventual paradise, whereas the final fate of a soul in
transmigration may still be hell. At this point the Aryan and Semitic
eschatologies do not entirely coincide.[1]

A revealing discrepancy between the Hindu and Buddhist theory
of a succession of births and deaths (for the unsanctified or unsaved
soul) and the fantastical reincarnationism of Western cults is that the
Hindu and the Buddhist strive at all costs to avoid "rebirth" (which
would be "peripheral", and in another world), whereas the pseudo-es-
oterist imprudently (and illusorily) hankers after a further life or lives
(which he imagines will be "central", and in *this* world). The Hindu
or Buddhist seeks to escape from the "round of existence"; the impi-
ous heretic longs to remain within it. For the Hindu or Buddhist there
could be no clearer proof of his perversity.

According to the Hindus and Buddhists, the chances of being "reborn" into a "central" state are minimal; it is said: "The human state
is hard to obtain." But more than that: the human state, by definition,
is the only escape route from the "round of existence"; it is thus the
threshold of Paradise. To squander this privilege, to miss one's only
opportunity of salvation, is the greatest possible folly and tragedy.

*
* *

Linked with transmigration is the doctrine of *karma* (the effect of
past actions). In Christianity, this doctrine is expressed in the verses:
"Whatsoever a man soweth, that shall he also reap" (Galatians, 6:7)
and "Vengeance is mine, saith the Lord, I will repay" (Romans, 12:19).
Buddhism, like the other religions, teaches that reward or retribution
can occur both in this life and posthumously. There is, however, an escape from the inexorable justice of *karma*: this lies in the saving truth
of the revealed doctrine, and in the saving efficacy of the revealed
means of grace (which are activated by faith and practice).

---

[1] See Frithjof Schuon, "Universal Eschatology", in *Survey of Metaphysics and Esoterism*
(Bloomington, IN: World Wisdom, 1985).

Some of those who have failed to understand the doctrine of *anātmā* (see pp. 43-46) have gone so far as to allege that Buddhism denies the existence of the soul. In point of fact, Buddhism takes enormous pains to emphasize "karmic continuity" or, in the words of Frithjof Schuon, "the moral causality of that living and conscious nucleus that is the [human] ego".[2] The numerous references in the Buddhist Scriptures to posthumous hells (the fate awaiting those who have squandered the precious gift of human life) cannot be lightly brushed aside.

*
*   *

The term "reincarnation" is sometimes used to describe the mechanism of Tibetan lamaist succession, for example, that of the Dalai Lamas. This is rather misleading, however, as in this case, it is the "office" or "function" (and not the individual) that is "reincarnated". It would be more accurate to say that the office or function is "bequeathed", "transmitted", or "passed on" to a traditionally chosen successor.

A twentieth-century Dalai Lama might well say: "As I said in 1600. . .". Here it is the office or function that is speaking. A Pope often says something like: "As my august predecessor said in 1600. . .". In Tibetan terms, he could just as well say: "As I said in 1600. . .". In such cases it is the office or function that is involved.

The perfume of flowers goes not against the wind, not even the perfume of sandalwood, rose-bay, or jasmine; but the perfume of virtue travels against the wind and reaches unto the ends of the earth.

Dhammapada, 54

---

[2] Frithjof Schuon, *Treasures of Buddhism*, p. 37.

Tai Chi, *Returning Late from a Spring Outing*, China, 15th century

At the horrible time of the end, men will be malevolent, false, evil, and obtuse and they will imagine that they have reached perfection when it will be nothing of the sort.

Saddharma-Pundarīka-Sūtra

(22) The Question of "Pantheism"

Very often the term "pantheism" is applied to Oriental doctrines, especially the metaphysical and/or mystical doctrines of Buddhism (both *Hīnayāna* and *Mahāyāna*), Vedānta, Taoism, and Sufism. The immediate and formal answer to this is that no traditional doctrine is pantheistic, since the vague, superficial, and contradictory notion of pantheism (a material or substantial identity between two different levels of reality) is a purely modern phenomenon.

What rescues all traditional doctrine, including Buddhist, from the charge of pantheism is, in a word, transcendence: Ultimate Reality is transcendent, and there is no material or substantial identity between Ultimate Reality and the manifested world (or between Creator and creation, as the "theistic" religions would say). This applies also in the case of Hindu and Greek "emanationism", in which the Principle remains wholly transcendent of any of its manifestations.

Of course all metaphysical or mystical doctrines (be they Oriental, Greek, or Christian) are doctrines of union. The metaphysicians and mystics of the great religions have referred to different degrees of union, notably ontological or supra-ontological, that is to say, relating either to the level of "Being" or "Beyond-Being". (See pp. 48, 50-51.) Christ said: "I and the Father are one", and the Christian way is essentially to unite oneself with Christ. In Hinduism, it is said that "all things are *Ātmā*". This means (and it is in accordance with the doctrine of Plato) that all things have their principle on a level of reality *above* the one on which they "exist", and that the Principle of principles is *Ātmā*. There is indeed "essential" identity, but there is "substantial" discontinuity.

In Hinduism it is also said: "The world is false, *Brahma* is true", while in Christianity it is said: "Heaven and earth shall pass away, but My words will not pass away." To allude to the ephemerality of all created things (something that has been known from time immemorial) is not pantheism, but simply true doctrine.

It is true that there are mystical and scriptural expressions (both Oriental and Christian) which use figures of material continuity, for example, when it is said that all creatures are vessels made from the same Clay, or that all rivers return to the one Ocean; or again, when Christ says: "I am the vine, ye are the branches." However, the symbolic nature of such utterances is perfectly clear, and in any case the traditional commentaries ensure that the principle of transcendence is fully safeguarded.

The idea of a material or substantial identity between two different levels of reality (or the obtuseness of taking literally any metaphor which might seem to suggest this) devolves on European philosophers and poets of recent centuries. The idea is far from reality and devoid of meaning; it is foreign to Buddhism and all other traditional perspectives.

Torii at Itsukushima Shrine, Miyajima, Hiroshima Prefecture, Japan

People find themselves drowning in a sea of accidents; they do not know how to reach the one substance which alone is truth.

Chiang Chih-chi

(23) Shinto: Buddhism's Partner in Japan

"The Way of the Gods" (Kami-no-Michi)

As mentioned on pp. 54 and 101, certain indigenous traditions (derivatives of Hyperborean shamanism) co-exist with Buddhism in some countries: Bön in Tibet, Confucianism and Taoism in China, and Shinto in Japan.

Buddhism and Shintoism have both permeated Japanese civilization, and anyone who takes an interest in Buddhism in Japan must also know something about *Shintō*, "the way of the Gods". That this is so is strongly and clearly confirmed by tradition, as the two following quotations show:

> This is the land of the Gods [Shintoism]. The people should revere them. In my essence, I am the Buddha Vairochana. Let my people understand this and take refuge in the Law of the Buddhas.
>
> *The Sun-Goddess Amaterasu*
> *to the Emperor Shōmu in 742 A.D.*

> There is nothing but the difference between the trough and the crest of a wave between what we call Gods [Shintoism] and what we call Buddhas.
>
> *Hakuin* (1683-1768)

While the two religious traditions remain distinct, there have been occasions where a Shintoist divinity could be assimilated to a Bodhisattva, since the essence of each was identical.

We have taken the following schematic outline of Shinto mythology from *Treasures of Buddhism* by Frithjof Schuon (section on Shinto, pp. 183-199). Here and there analogies are made with elements from Hindu metaphysics and cosmology which, as is so often the case, can serve as useful points of reference.

Schematic Summary of Shinto Mythology and Cosmology

For an explanation of the terms immediately below, see pp. 48, 50-51.

Ame-no-Minakanushi-no-Kami
("Divine Lord of the Center of the Heavens")
Ame-no-Tokotachi-no-Misoko
("The Majestic One who stands on
the Floor of the Sky")

"BEYOND-BEING"
(SUPRA-PERSONAL
GOD OR DIVINE
ESSENCE)

Kuni-Tokotachi-no-Mikoto
("Eternal Divine Earthly Being",
"He who eternally stands above the world")
Tsuchi-Tokotachi-no-Misoko
("The Majestic One who stands on the Floor of the Earth")

"BEING"
(PERSONAL GOD)

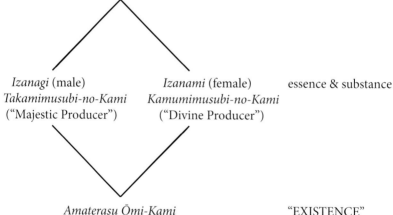

Izanagi (male)   *Izanami* (female)
Takamimusubi-no-Kami   *Kamumimusubi-no-Kami*
("Majestic Producer")   ("Divine Producer")

essence & substance

Amaterasu Ōmi-Kami
(Solar Goddess: "Great Divinity of the Shining Sky")
Ohiru-Memuchi-no-Kami
("She who possesses the Great Sun")
Hiruko
(Solar God: "Great Sun")

"EXISTENCE"
(*SAMSĀRA*)

Jimmu Tennō (founded Japanese Empire in 600 B.C.)

Alternative Schema

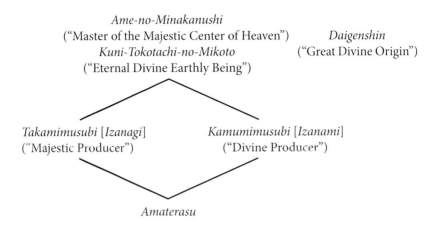

Ame-no-Minakanushi
("Master of the Majestic Center of Heaven")   Daigenshin
Kuni-Tokotachi-no-Mikoto   ("Great Divine Origin")
("Eternal Divine Earthly Being")

Takamimusubi [Izanagi]   Kamumimusubi [Izanami]
("Majestic Producer")   ("Divine Producer")

Amaterasu

"The Three Noble Children of Izanagi"

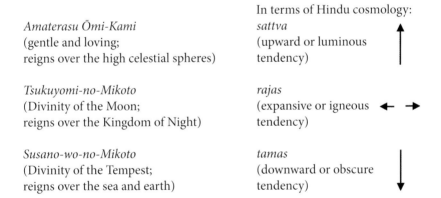

	In terms of Hindu cosmology:
Amaterasu Ōmi-Kami (gentle and loving; reigns over the high celestial spheres)	sattva (upward or luminous tendency)
Tsukuyomi-no-Mikoto (Divinity of the Moon; reigns over the Kingdom of Night)	rajas (expansive or igneous tendency)
Susano-wo-no-Mikoto (Divinity of the Tempest; reigns over the sea and earth)	tamas (downward or obscure tendency)

Yet Another Cosmogonic Schema

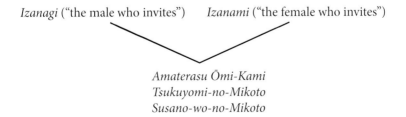

Izanagi ("the male who invites")   Izanami ("the female who invites")

Amaterasu Ōmi-Kami
Tsukuyomi-no-Mikoto
Susano-wo-no-Mikoto

Some Further Proper Names from Shinto Mythology

Yomotsu-kuni   "Land of Darkness"
("female who invites"):

Yaso-Maga-Tsu-Hi: "Genius of Multiple Calamities"

Kamu-Nahobi: "Genius of Reparations"

Kagutsuchi ("Radiant One")/   "Son of Izanami"
Homusubi ("He who engenders Fire"):

Ukemochi: "Goddess of Sustenance"

Ama-no-Hashidate: Bridge linking Heaven and Earth

Onokoro: "Self-congealed" (Island of Japan)

Hiru-ko: "Leech-son" of Izanagi and Izanami

A Shinto mirror, symbol of Amaterasu

Ise Jingu's Inner Shrine, which houses the sacred mirror of Shintoism, Naiku, Mie Prefecture, Japan

Screen with gingko tree, early Edo period, Japan, 17th century

Gāte, gāte; pāragāte; pārasamgāte; Bodhi, svāhā!

Departed, departed; departed for the other shore; arrived at the other shore; O Enlightenment, be blessed!

Prajñā-Pāramitā-Hridaya-Sūtra

The use by adepts of this famous *mantra* from the *Prajñā-Pāramitā-Hridaya-Sūtra* is said to engender assimilation with the *Vajrakāya* ("Diamond Body"), which is a synonym for the *Dharmakāya* ("Universal Body"). See p. 50.

Vajrayāna = Tantrayāna = Mantrayāna

Buddhist eternal knot motif

SELECT BIBLIOGRAPHY

Ballou, Robert (ed.). *The Bible of the World*. London: Kegan Paul/New York: Avon Books, 1940.

Basham, A.L. *The Wonder That was India*. London: Fontana/New York: Grove Press, 1954.

Burckhardt, Titus. "The Image of the Buddha" and "Landscape in Far-Eastern Art". In *Sacred Art in East and West*. Bloomington, IN: World Wisdom, 2001. Two major studies.

Conze, Edward. *Buddhism: Its Essence and Development*. Oxford: Cassirer/New York: Harper & Row, 1951.
———. *Buddhist Scriptures*. Baltimore: Penguin Books, 1959.

Coomaraswamy, Ananda. *Elements of Buddhist Iconography*. Cambridge, MA: Harvard University Press, 1935.
———. *Hinduism and Buddhism*. New York: Philosophical Library, 1943.
———. *The Living Thoughts of Gotama the Buddha*. London: Cassell, 1948.
——— & Sister Nivedita. *Myths of the Hindus and Buddhists*. London: Harrap, 1913.

Harrer, Heinrich. *Seven Years in Tibet*. London: Pan Books, 1953.

Herrigel, Eugen. *Zen in the Art of Archery*. London: Kegan Paul/New York: Random House, 1953.
———. *The Method of Zen*. London: Kegan Paul/New York: Random House, 1960.

Herrigel, Gustie. *Zen in the Art of Flower Arrangement*. London: Kegan Paul, 1958.

Hōnen the Buddhist Saint, edited by Joseph A. Fitzgerald. Bloomington, IN: World Wisdom, 2006.

Horner, I.B. "Dhamma in Early Buddhism". In *The Unanimous Tradition*, edited by Ranjit Fernando. Colombo: Sri Lanka Institute of Traditional Studies, 1991.

Inagaki, Hisao & Harold Stewart. *The Three Pure Land Sūtras.* Kyoto: Nagata Bunshodo, 1995.

Life of Milarepa, The, translated by Lhobsang P. Lhalungpa. New York: Dutton, 1977.

Masefield, Peter. *Divine Revelation in Pali Buddhism.* London: Routledge, 2008.

Okakura, Kakuzo. *The Book of Tea.* Rutland, VT: Charles E. Tuttle Company, 1906.

Pallis, Marco. *Peaks and Lamas.* London: Frank Cass, 1974.
———. *A Buddhist Spectrum.* Bloomington IN: World Wisdom, 2003.
———. *The Way and the Mountain.* Bloomington, IN: World Wisdom, 2008.

Schuon, Frithjof. *Treasures of Buddhism.* Bloomington, IN: World Wisdom, 1993. [Revised and enlarged edition of *In the Tracks of Buddhism.*] The best explanation of Buddhism available.

Shastri, Hari Prasad. *Echoes of Japan.* London: Shanti Sadan, 1961.

Stein, R.A. *Tibetan Civilization.* London: Faber, 1972.

Steinilber, E. & Kuni Matsuo. *Les Sectes Bouddhiques Japonaises.* Paris: Crès, 1930.

Stewart, Harold. *A Net of Fireflies* [Japanese *haiku* and *haiku* paintings with verse translations by Harold Stewart]. Rutland, VT/Tokyo, Japan: Charles E. Tuttle Company, 1960.

Suzuki, Daisetz Teitaro. *Outlines of Mahāyāna Buddhism.* London: Luzac & Co., 1907.
———. *Introduction to Zen Buddhism.* New York: Causeway Books, 1974.

Tibet's Great Yogī Milarepa: A Biography from the Tibetan, edited by W.Y. Evans-Wentz. Oxford: Oxford University Press, 2000.

INDEX

For a glossary of all key foreign words used in books published by World
Wisdom, including metaphysical terms in English, consult:
www.DictionaryofSpiritualTerms.org.
This on-line Dictionary of Spiritual Terms provides extensive definitions,
examples, and related terms in other languages.

BIOGRAPHICAL NOTES

William Stoddart was born in Carstairs, Scotland, lived most of his life in London, England, and now lives in Windsor, Ontario. He studied modern languages, and later medicine, at the universities of Glasgow, Edinburgh, and Dublin. He was a close associate of both Frithjof Schuon and Titus Burckhardt during the lives of these leading perennialists and translated several of their works into English. For many years Stoddart was also assistant editor of the British journal *Studies in Comparative Religion*. Pursuing his interests in comparative religion, he has traveled widely in Europe, North Africa, India, Sri Lanka, and Japan. Stoddart's works include *Outline of Hinduism* (1993; 2007 edition titled *Hinduism and Its Spiritual Masters*), *Outline of Buddhism* (1998), *Outline of Sufism: The Essentials of Islamic Spirituality* (2012), *Invincible Wisdom: Quotations from the Scriptures, Saints, and Sages of All Times and Places* (2008), *What Do the Religions Say About Each Other? Christian Attitudes towards Islam, Islamic Attitudes towards Christianity* (2008), and *What Does Islam Mean in Today's World?* (2012). His essential writings were published by World Wisdom as *Remembering in a World of Forgetting: Thoughts on Tradition and Postmodernism* (2008).

Joseph A. Fitzgerald studied Comparative Religion at Indiana University, where he also earned a Doctor of Jurisprudence degree. For over twenty years he has traveled extensively throughout the Buddhist world, including visits to Bhutan, Mongolia, Cambodia, Burma, Thailand, Nepal, India, and Japan. He is an award-winning editor whose previous publications include *Honen the Buddhist Saint: Essential Writings and Official Biography* (2006), *The Essential Sri Anandamayi Ma: Life and Teachings of a 20th Century Saint from India* (2007), *The Way and the Mountain: Tibet, Buddhism, and Tradition* (2008), *An Illustrated Introduction to Taoism: The Wisdom of the Sages* (2010), *The Original Gospel of Ramakrishna* (2011), and *The Wisdom of Ananda Coomaraswamy* (with S.D.R. Singam) (2011). Joseph lives with his wife and daughters in Bloomington, Indiana.

World Wisdom Titles on Buddhism

The Buddha Eye:
An Anthology of the Kyoto School and Its Contemporaries,
edited by Frederick Franck, 2004

A Buddhist Spectrum: Contributions to Buddhist-Christian Dialogue,
by Marco Pallis, 2004

The Essential Shinran: A Buddhist Path of True Entrusting,
edited by Alfred Bloom, 2007

The Golden Age of Zen: Zen Masters of the T'ang Dynasty,
by John C.H. Wu, 2004

Honen the Buddhist Saint: Essential Writings and Official Biography,
edited by Joseph A. Fitzgerald, 2006

An Illustrated Outline of Buddhism:
The Essentials of Buddhist Spirituality,
by William Stoddart, 2013

The Laughing Buddha of Tofukuji:
The Life of Zen Master Keido Fukushima,
by Ishwar Harris, 2004

Living in Amida's Universal Vow: Essays in Shin Buddhism,
edited by Alfred Bloom, 2004

Naturalness: A Classic of Shin Buddhism,
by Kenryo Kanamatsu, 2002

Samdhong Rinpoche: Uncompromising Truth for a
Compromised World: Tibetan Buddhism and Today's World,
edited by Donovan Roebert, 2006

Treasures of Buddhism,
by Frithjof Schuon, 1993

The Way and the Mountain: Tibet, Buddhism, and Tradition,
by Marco Pallis, 2008

Zen Buddhism: A History, Vol. 1: India and China,
by Heinrich Dumoulin, 2005

Zen Buddhism: A History, Vol. 2: Japan,
by Heinrich Dumoulin, 2005